Narrative Innovation
and Political Change
in Mexico

University of Texas Studies in Contemporary Spanish-American Fiction

Robert Brody
General Editor

Vol. 4

PETER LANG
New York • Bern • Frankfurt am Main • Paris

John S. Brushwood

Narrative Innovation
and Political Change
in Mexico

for Merlin,
with the usual high regard,
John

PETER LANG
New York • Bern • Frankfurt am Main • Paris

Library of Congress Cataloging-in-Publication
Data

Brushwood, John Stubbs
    Narrative innovation and political change in
Mexico / John S. Brushwood.
        p. cm. — (University of Texas studies in
contemporary Spanish-American fiction ; vol. 4)
        Bibliography: p.
    1. Mexican fiction—20th century—History and
criticism.   2. Politics and literature—Mexico.   I.
Title.   II. Series.
PQ7203.B77   1989   863—dc20   89-31589
ISBN 0-8204-0966-9   CIP
ISSN 0888-8787

CIP-Titelaufnahme der Deutschen Bibliothek

Brushwood, John S.:
Narrative innovation and political change in
Mexico / John S. Brushwood. — New York;
Bern; Frankfurt am Main; Paris: Lang, 1989.
    (University of Texas Studies in Contemporary
    Spanish-American Fiction; Vol. 4)
    ISBN 0-8204-0966-9

NE: University of Texas <Austin, Tex. >:
University of Texas . . .

© Peter Lang Publishing, Inc., New York 1989

Printed by Weihert-Druck GmbH, Darmstadt, West Germany

Criticism cannot assume that its province is merely the text, nor even the great literary text. It must see itself, as well as other discourse, inhabiting a much contested cultural space in which what has counted in the continuity and transmission of knowledge has been the signifier as an event that has left lasting traces upon the human subject. Once we take that view, then literature as an isolated paddock in the broad cultural field disappears, and with it too the harmless rhetoric of self-delighting humanism. Instead we will be able, I think, to read and write with a sense of the greater stake in historical and political effectiveness that literary, as well as other, texts have had.

Edward W. Said, "The Problem of Textuality: Two Exemplary Positions."

Contents

Preface

This study was engendered by a lecture entitled "Literary Nostalgia and Economic Disaster," delivered at the University of Texas-Austin, in October, 1984, and later published in *The Mexican Forum*, in April, 1985. Some observations I had made about recent Mexican fiction prompted me to propose, at least half in jest, that novels might be used as prognosticators of future public policy. While my research since that time would not prompt me to move from suggestion to categorical affirmation, it very clearly indicates a relationship between fiction and politics that is quite different from the common assumption that novels are a reflection of what has already become obvious in other social phenomena.

Some approach to this idea has been operative in my thinking for many years. In 1964, I began the Preface of *Mexico in its Novel* with a statement concerning the relationship of the novel to society (ix). Since that time, my analytical procedures — or, to put it less elegantly: the way I read novels — have undergone several changes influenced by waves of theory teasing the shores of literary scholarship. My readers will most likely note the effect of several theoreticians; however, it should be understood that I do not intend to base my analyses on any particular theory or method. Ideas gleaned from the books of others have been very useful to me; systems have not proved so helpful. One preoccupation has been constant throughout my research: the sense that novels perform social functions not generally recognized by literary scholars, and certainly not considered by anyone outside the field of literature.

The initial stage of this project involved identifying periods of obvious innovation in Mexican narrative and, at the same time, stating a basic proposition that might serve as a rationale for what I was undertaking. The first of these tasks was rather easily accomplished, and the periods of innovation are represented in the first three chapters of the study. One deals with the innovations (many of them called "vanguardist") during the nineteen-twenties and nineteen-thirties. It soon became apparent, in dealing with this material, that a return to an earlier period would be needed for clarification; therefore, the chapter refers back to a time before the Revolution, and even into nineteenth-century *modernismo*. The second chapter deals with a period of innovation at approximately mid-century that is identified by internationalism in narrative strategies, and paradoxically, internationalism (or better, universality) in dealing with nationalistic themes. This is the period that saw the rise of the "new novel." Chapter Three includes the nineteen-sixties and nineteen-seventies, but is focussed especially on the experimentation and dissidence of the middle and later sixties. These three chapters are presented in chronological order; the fourth, on the nineteenth-century, is not in sequence. It has some qualities of background information, but it works better as I have placed it, because some of the findings are at odds with the generalities that are common to the chapters on the twentieth century. Each chapter is written so it can be read independently; for that reason, some repetitions may be noticed.

As for the statement of a rationale, one begins with the knowledge that Spanish-Americanists have long recognized the close relationship between literature and society in their field, usually with emphasis on narrative fiction. With this fact in mind, one may formulate a question about moments of change in literature and society. It is fairly obvious that narrative would provide a firmer basis than the other literary genres (certainly, all could be significant) and politics or public policy would provide a fairly certain handle for understanding social change.

I propose, then, the coincidence of innovation/change in two different constituent elements of society. Such an assumption does not necessarily mean that change in one causes change in the other. Nevertheless, it seems reasonable to suppose that some kind of relationship exists, probably as a common response to a more general phenomenon. Such a motivating force might be identified simply as frustration — frustration born of human failure to exercise the creative faculties inherent in the human condition.

Such a condition must produce, from time to time, a sense of stasis. Even if one rejects the possibility of a completely static society, it is clearly admissible that an illusion of stasis could arise from a relatively static condition. In such a circumstance, one or another constituent element of society will initiate a change. Other constituents follow, not in imitation, but in response to the same circumstance. Given the creative, imaginative, quality of the arts, it seems probable that one or another artistic medium may make the earliest response to the sense of stasis. However, there is no other inherent reason for one constituent element preceding another in innovation. It is important that the process be understood as holistic; even as our sense of chronology causes us to see the response as diachronic, the metaphoric nature of the responses should be understood.

Three matters of a linguistic nature call for some comment. First, English versions of originally Spanish quotations are mine unless otherwise indicated. The second matter, considerably more complicated, has to do with the word "narrative." I have in mind narratives that we ordinarily think of as fiction. I am aware that not all narratives are fictions, at least in the usual sense; I am also aware that the degree of fictionality (or of transformation) is variable. The present study is not concerned with these questions; rather, it assumes a common acceptance of "narrative" as referring to the text(s) we read and usually refer to as "novel" or "short story." My "narrative" is Gérard Genette's *récit*. The third point: I retain the Spanish *modernista* to refer to the literature and period generally assigned that term in Hispanic studies; the English "modernism" is used for reference to the phenomena so designated by scholars in other literatures. My opinion is that these terms are not mutually exclusive, but neither are they synonymous.

Some of the material contained in Chapter One appears in abbreviated form in the Winter, 1989 issue of *Mexican Studies/ Estudios Mexicanos*.

I offer my sincere thanks to many people who have made this study possible. A few names seem especially in order: Carolyn Brushwood, always my first reader and the silent partner in my research; Jon Vincent, whose interest and expertise in area studies enabled him to read these chapters with the necessary critical eye; Merlin Forster, who was responsible for the invitation that triggered this project. Very special thanks are due the Rockefeller Foundation for five weeks of residence at the Bellagio Study and Conference Center, where the final chapter and the conclusions were written.

General Editor's Note

The reader will realize soon into John Brushwood's book that some portions of it focus on topics apparently outside the scope of what scholars of Spanish-American fiction understand as the contemporary period. In a strict sense, this is true. It is also true that his discussion of vanguardism in Chapter One and nineteenth-century fiction in Chapter Four serve effectively as pointers to highlight, clarify and otherwise call attention to the veritable heart of Brushwood's book — the analysis of contemporary Mexican fiction in the light of its relationship to politics, as presented in Chapters Two and Three.

Chapter 1

Revolution and Vanguardism
(1910-1934)

In an essay on the vanguardist painter, Carlos Mérida, Patty Koeniger writes, "Mérida represents the middle of the road stance in American painting: wanting neither to be purely nationalistic ... and separate from the mainstream of art, nor, on the other hand, only modern, concerned only with the European schools" (Koeniger 7). If it seems strange that an essay on fiction and politics should begin with reference to a painter, the choice can be explained by taking Mérida as a sort of metaphor of his time; the bipolarity confronting him was faced by artists in all genres, and the meaning of "nationalism" is clarified by the fact that Mérida was a Guatemalan by birth though he worked mainly in Mexico, so "nationalism" can be understood, in some contexts, as "nativism" or *indigenismo*. A similar condition might well be attributed to Mexican politics during this period, a time of seeking an appropriate direction in both politics and narrative.

Farther along in her essay, Koeniger says, "We do not know exactly why Mérida became an internationalist rather than an *indigenista*" (Koeniger 10). This observation, too, speaks eloquently to the circumstance of the period. The "why" of the road taken by certain writers is equally uncertain, and the trajectory of politics is no more easily understood. It seems possible that a study of innovation in narrative fiction, along with speculation concerning its analogy to politics, may enhance our understanding of a complex and extremely significant period in Mexican culture; that is, culture in the larger sense, not simply the fine arts.

When we speak of the Mexican Revolution, we think of a series of armed struggles that lasted from 1910 until 1917, when the new constitution was promulgated and Venustiano Carranza was well established as president of the republic, his period in office extending from 1916 to 1920. We also think of a subsequent period of social change that is marked by the literacy campaign, by José Vasconcelos' promotion of the classics, by the work of the great muralists, by so-called "vanguardism" in literature, by the Chávez school of music, by the most intense of Mexico's church/state crises, by the promise of agrarian reform, by a series of political assassinations, and possibly by other equally significant specifics that function in individual repertories. It was undoubtedly a remarkable period in Mexico, possibly better characterized by a general sense of potential well being than by reference to specific phenomena. Daniel Cosío Villegas has written to that effect. In his *Change in Latin America*, he says that by 1920, the Revolution was popularly accepted, morale was high, and both the government and the country as a whole enjoyed a feeling of self-confidence: "Not 'everybody' but certainly large numbers everywhere felt that exalted sensation of man turned into a god, of man with creative genius and will, with the faith that from his hands may come a new, great, brilliant, harmonious and kind world; faith, also, that nothing is impossible and that anything may be achieved by simply willing it" (Cosío V. 29).

The problem was the extent to which this energy should be channeled into nationalistic concerns and expression, as against a more cosmopolitan position. It is important to notice that the problem was one of degree, not a matter of categorical choice. Nationalism versus cosmopolitanism constitutes an axiomatic opposition, in theory. Nevertheless, in practice, even though the opposition remains a fact, the two opposites do exist at the same time, in the same place, and even as factors in the same enterprise. Take for example the *colonialista* novels, a kind of narrative that flourished from 1918 to 1926. Their subject matter tends to be anecdotal, tales of Mexico's Colonial Period. The language may be described as feigned archaic. Unquestionably, a nationalistic impulse

was at work in them; the stories deal with the national past, characterize extraordinary historical personages, develop a sense of
this-is-where-we-came-from. This awareness of identity is itself
multifaceted. The notion of retreat to the Colonial Period suggests
a desire to get away from the confusion of revolutionary Mexico; at
the same time, the retreat itself enhances the sense of belonging to
a tradition. The novels also communicate some of the feeling that
one enjoys on visiting a recognized historical spot: a special, almost
possessive consciousness of the place, of being where an important
event actually happened (Brushwood 1966, 185-187). The *colonialistas* very clearly emphasized the Hispanic heritage. This quality
indicates not only a continued relationship with Europe, but also a
reaffirmation of relationship with Spain. (France had been the
predominant European influence in Mexico from the time of the
Independence.) In addition, these novels counterbalance post-
Revolutionary emphasis on the indigenous Mexicans. Cosío
Villegas says that during the "good years" of the Revolution
(1920-1925), it was thought that the Mexican Indian could be
brought into the modern world without destroying the values of his
traditional way of life (Cosío V. 34). It is obvious that, precisely
during these good years, the innovative *colonialista* novel was
making a different kind of statement, one that expressed pride in
the Hispanic heritage. It is also interesting to note, in this connection, John Johnson's study of decision-making by the "urban middle
sectors". He points out that these sectors held on tenaciously during the period of radical agrarianism following the Revolution, and
finally returned to predominance during the nineteen-forties
(Johnson 128 ff.). Undoubtedly, the *colonialista* writers were announcing the persistence of the urban middle sectors, as did innovative narrative throughout the years between the Revolution and
the decade of the forties; in fact, the words "innovative fiction"
could be satisfactorily substituted for "urban middle sectors", in
Johnson's statement. But such a view into the future is less important than a look backward from the innovations of the *colonialistas*,
for the immediate purposes of this essay.

An understanding of innovation in narrative and politics during this period depends on an explanation of the Ateneo de la Juventud as a revolutionary force, and even certain aspects of *modernismo*. It is generally agreed -- by José Luis Martínez, Alfonso Reyes, Samuel Ramos, José Rojas Garcidueñas, among others -- that the activities of the Ateneo anticipated the political revolution. It was the intellectual side of the Revolution, so to speak, especially because of its rejection of Positivism as the philosophical guide of Mexican culture. Rojas Garcidueñas, via a remarkable quotation of Alfonso Reyes, provides a vicarious experience of that time, as only a poet can do, referring to interests other than the defeat of Positivism, recognizing the coming political upheaval, and communicating the excitement of change. As an all too brief example: "That generation of young people was educated among philosophical discussions that were to be throttled by the thunder of revolution. What happened in Mexico, in the Centenary Year of Independence, was like a shot in the deceptive silence of a polar landscape; the circle of glacial mountains came down completely, falling one after the other" (Rojas G. 1979, 109. This quotation is not specifically identified, although the book is otherwise carefully documented.)

The "circle of glacial mountains" refers, of course, to the stasis of the Porfirio Díaz dictatorship. It is possible to argue interminably as to whether a truly static society can exist, but it is preferable to understand "stasis" as the slowing of a flow, rather than a perfectly static condition. Evelyn Picón-Garfield and Ivan A. Schulman explain that stasis does not prohibit variety (72-75), and this condition certainly describes that of fiction and of politics during the Díaz regime, though one could argue about the point in history at which the condition began. Picón-Garfield and Schulman prefer a date earlier than that favored, for example, by Leonard B. Meyer, who seems to refer to that ill-defined condition we call "postmodernism" (89-103). On the other hand, Paul Kecskemeti says that, since the Renaissance, humankind has been increasingly dynamic, and that the comfort of a static society must be sacrificed for higher values (39-40). One could hardly find a better general statement of the Ateneo's reaction against the old regime.

Johnson writes that, by 1910, education had deteriorated "to the point where Mexico was referred to as a 'cultural desert'" (129). On the face of it, this assertion seems strange, since it refers to the period when the art-for-art's-sake enterprise of *modernismo* flourished. Then one recalls that the masters of this literary promotion were French, and not always the most up-to-date French writers at that. In fact, the Gallic quality of this period in Mexico tended to be static. Even the architecture seems to present a given concept of French style, rather than a dynamic pursuit of change in French taste. The change that one notes is the movement from Hispanic taste toward predominance of the French. One finds little that can be called "nativistic." At the same time, the Díaz government depended less and less on a large segment of Mexican support among intellectuals and/or businessmen, preferring a small group of Mexican power-brokers known as the *científicos*, along with foreign investors. Johnson believes that this policy produced an alliance between intellectuals who found no opportunity to exercise their ability and businessmen who must have felt equally isolated. He believes that anti-foreign sentiment began at that point (128-131).

Modernismo was certainly not a Mexican tradition in opposition to the establishment, but some aspects of it reveal a deep current of doubt if not of dissatisfaction. In the most general sense, while some may choose to look at art-for-art's-sake as an escapist impulse, others may find in it a protest against a prevailing situation that the artist rejects. Understood this way, *modernismo* anticipates that move toward higher values taken by both literature and politics in the rupture that we call the "Revolution."

More specifically in some works of fiction, one can find experimental combinations of theme and technique that project a sense of uneasiness, of anticipation of change. Manuel Gutiérrez Nájera's "Rip-Rip" employs a variety of narrative techniques — indirect free style, untagged dialogue, negation of logical time — to raise questions about human relationships and, by implication, about the significance of the past/present differentiation and the viability of what is not "modern." Amado Nervo, in *Pascual Aguilera* and *El bachiller*, uses narrative material from the Mexican literary repertory; one is a treatment of the *hacendado's* right to possess the peasant bride on her wedding night, the other deals with clerical celibacy. Both narratives show dissatisfaction with the social phenomena they describe; both novels make use of the "new science" of their day, psychology; both are short and carefully focused, as a short story might be, or a modern lyric poem.

Even more innovative was Nervo's third novelette, *El donador de almas*, first published in 1899. This narrative is an early science fiction, based on parapsychology, in which a physician — practical, scientific, and bored — is given a soul by his poet friend. The story anticipates the rejection of Positivism by the intellectual community, and the ousting of Díaz and the "científicos" in the political realm. *El donador de almas* is innovative not only in theme, but in narrative strategy as well. Nervo uses a minimum of intrusion by the explicatory voice within the scenes of the story (that is, there is a minimum of "telling" in the midst of "showing"), and he uses supposed newspaper accounts to avoid excessive narrative summary. On the other hand, the author, as author, intrudes to comment on the making of the narrative and, at the end of the story, there is a dialogued discussion of its significance and how it was made, including a defense of the *nouvelle* as a genre. This last feature looks forward to the emphasis on process that is necessarily a characteristic of politics following the Revolution, and also to a similar interest in process that is apparent in the self-conscious narrative of the nineteen-twenties and, of course, the novel of the late twentieth century.

The Ateneo de la Juventud was an intellectual renovation, not primarily literary. Its founding, in October of 1909, was not exactly an unprecedented phenomenon; various investigators find antecedents in the earlier years of the twentieth century: the magazine *Savia Moderna*, the Sociedad de Conferencias, Justo Sierra's speech, in 1908, in which he paid homage to Gabino Barreda, but expressed doubt concerning Barreda's hope of perfecting society through science. However, the Ateneo's greatest effect was produced by its members' concern, conscious or subconscious, for Mexico's identity in an international context. As for Positivism, a series of six lectures by Antonio Caso, in 1909, further weakened its hold on intellectuals, and the Ateneo marked its end. In this regard, Mexico was certainly not alone; José Enrique Rodo's famous essay, *Ariel*, is comparable to the influence of the Ateneo (Ramos 82).

José Luis Martínez points out two basic goals of the Ateneo: (1) the definition of a set of appropriate interests for Mexican intellectuals, and (2) a disciplined approach to cultural activity. Regarding the first, he mentions interest in specifically Mexican culture, in Spanish and English literature as well as in French, in new critical methods of analyzing literature and philosophy, in universal thought, and in interdisciplinary relationships. Regarding the second, Martínez says that, oversimplifying but in a meaningful way, the writers suddenly went from the bohemian life to their libraries/studies (Martínez 4-5).

Rojas Garcidueñas provides a good account of the Ateneo lectures in 1910, the Centenary year (1979, 79-108); the titles alone give a reasonably clear idea of the group's orientation: Antonio Caso on "La filosofía moral de Hostos," Alfonso Reyes on "Los poemas rústicos de Othón," Pedro Henríquez Ureña on "La obra de José Enrique Rodo," Carlos González Peña on "El Pensador Mexicano y su tiempo," José Escofet on "Sor Juana Inés de la Cruz," and José Vasconcelos on "Don Gabino Barreda y las ideas contemporáneas." While this was the Ateneo's most spectacular series, its members continued to meet, on a weekly basis, for lectures and discussions, until the group was dispersed by differing political positions during the military phase of the Revolution. As an intellectual group, the Ateneo proposed to bring Mexico into the twentieth century, just as the political side of the Revolution intended a corresponding advance. Indeed, the national/cosmopolitan bilateralism of the Ateneo looked into the future toward a position that the political sector would eventually have to take, after many years of seeking an appropriate path.

Of the *ateneístas*, Julio Torri is the most interesting for a study of prose fiction. Serge Zaitzeff, probably the most thorough analyst of Torri's work, says, "...since he finds the customary literary forms inadequate, Torri leans especially toward the prose poem and the short essay" (Zaitzeff 1980, 9). It is not always easy to distinguish between these two genres in Torri's work. Some of the pieces are characterized by a strong narrative factor which would not necessarily be indicated by the terms Zaitzeff uses and which are based on Torri's own classification. On the other hand, the importance of the narrative factor varies greatly from one piece to another, and it is precisely the freedom signified by such variety that constitutes innovation in Torri's work. He is very modern in that "he finds the customary literary forms inadequate" (Zaitzeff 1980, 9).

Both irony and brevity increase in Torri's later work, but with regard even to the very early pieces, Zaitzeff points to irony and also to the author's insistence that the apparently unreal (a dialogue between books) is not an invention but reality (13-14). It should be noted that this bibliothecal conversation does not project the fey charm of some *modernista* prose, but is more in the intellectual vein of Borges. Torri's innovations relate to other phenomena, artistic and political, in two different ways: (1) as a rupture of conventional limits on the form of expression, and (2) as an acknowledgment that art is an elitist activity.

With regard to literary form — that is, with regard to generic definition — Torri seems to abhor completeness (Zaitzeff 1983, 30-31). This preference is entirely in accord with some definitions of modernism, even though Torri expresses admiration for certain nineteenth-century writers. It is helpful, in this connection, to look briefly at painting. In her significantly titled book, *Diego Rivera: The Shaping of an Artist (1889-1921)*, Florence Arquin points out the importance of José María Velasco in the formation of Rivera, because the great landscapist subordinated the "severe, incisive line" that Rivera had been taught at the Academy of San Carlos (Arquin 13). Rivera was ready to rebel against the photographic realism of his academic masters and, indeed, combined his artistic restlessness with his political displeasure by leading a student strike, in 1902, protesting (1) the reelection of Porfirio Díaz and (2) the straitjacket instruction in the Academy of San Carlos. That same year, Dr. Atl (Gerardo Murillo) returned from Paris. Rivera himself went to France in 1909 and there completed his transition into modern painting before returning to Mexico. This movement away from the completeness of photographic realism seems quite similar to Torri's preference for brevity that promoted suggestion rather than definitiveness.

What was happening in the cases of Rivera and Dr. Atl certainly did not correspond to the political circumstance of the Díaz regime, but rather anticipated its collapse. Even more, it anticipated the political structure — or anti-structure — beyond the presidency of Francisco A. Madero, since the Madero period brought about some changes in the decision makers, but really did not succeed in eliminating the "severe, incisive line" of the establishment. Julio Torri's narrative innovation, right at the time of the Madero revolt, anticipates the post-Madero political situation (and post-Huerta) with respect to the breaking of traditional form. At the same time, Torri's work communicated the notion of elitism, a proposition that looks beyond those "good years" of the Revolution that Cosío Villegas identifies.

Torri admitted to an elitist appreciation of art, not in the sense of cultivating injustice toward any given group, but because he thought that art naturally distinguishes itself from the commonplace (Zaitzeff 1980, 9). This exclusivist (probably a better word that "elitist") attitude no doubt existed in all innovative writing, since one can hardly practice innovative narration without taking such a position. On the other hand, it seems that, among the *colonialista* writers, exclusivism existed also as a hedge against the populist, proletarian, or *indigenista* tendencies of the post-Revolutionary governments, especially in the "good years." Understanding the role of *colonialista* narrative is complicated by the fact that this particular phenomenon was not confined to Mexico. José Luis Martínez points out that it existed in Spain and in Argentina (18). It also coincides with the promotion of mission-style architecture in the United States and elsewhere. Nevertheless, its function in

Mexico seems more closely related to the social and political changes that were taking place.

The story material of these narratives emphasizes the Hispanic tradition even more than the Ateneo did. Although the *ateneístas* paid relatively little attention to popular or indigenous culture, they did emphasize a certain national interest, as in the lectures on Fernández de Lizardi, Sor Juana Inés de la Cruz, and Manuel José Othón. The difference in emphasis is caused largely by the *colonialistas'* use of Spanish that provided a certain flavor of the Colonial Period, a narrative strategy that corresponds to renewed awareness of the Spanish heritage. And of course, it contributed to the Mexican intellectuals' renewed interest in Spain. This special use of language is clearly that most innovative aspect of colonialist narrative; it also became its worst enemy, because its quaintness wore thin very rapidly. The language of the *colonialista* novels was only a simulation, and this condition may well be shared by other cultural phenomena that appear analogous to it. Genaro Estrada's *Pero Galín* (1926) is a *colonialista* novel that satirizes the genre and put an end to it as a literary enterprise, though one of its practitioners, Artemio de Valle Arizpe, was able to continue writing this kind of fiction with some success. Rojas Garciadueñas discussed the brief life of this subgenre in a tribute to Francisco Monterde in 1968. He made the point that its short life span does not diminish its importance as a factor in the national culture, and specifically recognized its role in identifying twentieth-century Mexicans with their colonial heritage (Rojas G. 1969).

Rojas Garciadueñas' tribute is a paper read on an occasion celebrating the fiftieth anniversary of Monterde's *El madrigal de Cetina* (1918), one of the earliest *colonialista* novels. This short narrative (sixty-eight pages in an edition commemorating its original publication) exemplifies the subgenre's essential characteristics. It refers to a supposed episode in the life of the Spanish poet, Gutierre de Cetina, when he was in Mexico. Specifically, it is based on his famous madrigal that begins, "Ojos claros, serenos" (Limpid, tranquil eyes). The narrator begins with an "Envoi" to the lady who has those "ojos claros, serenos," addressing her with the second-person, plural pronoun and verb, an archaic form of address that establishes the desired feeling of an epoch long past. He provides background information about the protagonists, a Spanish poet/soldier and a mestizo lady who, sure enough, has the "ojos claros" ("claros" carries the connotation of "light-colored") of her conquistador father and the bluish black hair of her mother, an Indian princess. This young woman, Maria Soledad, experiences great ambivalence as she observes the displacement of her mother's culture by her father's. Nevertheless, she accepts the desirability or inevitability of such a change, and learns to pray to the Holy Virgin for her own indigenous mother who died in childbirth. It is important to note that this absent mother is the only indigenous factor in the novel. What we know about Maria Soledad places her safely within the romantic tradition of literary *indianismo*, rather than the socially oriented *indigenismo*. The story that follows this introduction need not be told for present purposes. It is enough to say that Cetina's madrigal becomes a part of the story, the hero's destiny is left undetermined, and there is very slight characterization.

While the narrator gives some description of the people, they never seem more than shadows. This condition is characteristic of innovative novels in the nineteen-twenties, whether *colonialista* or of some other persuasion. Brevity and indeterminacy are also common. It seems strange to find them in a narrative as tradition-oriented as Monterde's; on the other hand, this tension between tradition and innovation is almost a definition of the period. It seems clear that the *colonialista* novel, flourishing at a time when populism briefly dominated the political scene, forecast a necessary balancing of the equation.

We must remember that Mariano Azuela, in an entirely different kind of novel, broke with traditional form at about the time of the Ateneo and continued experimenting with narrative technique in several subsequent novels, though he cannot be placed in any group, and often expressed disdain for any narrative that was not representational and without artistic pretensions. The case of Azuela is important because one often assumes that any novel that deals with the social/political realm will resemble a novel of Realism. This assumption is quite unfounded, and Azuela's *Los de abajo* is an excellent example. Its innovative characteristics may well be the result of a subconscious instinct that created a strategy appropriate to the subject matter. It certainly does not resemble the realist-naturalist novels that Azuela had been writing. Porfirio Díaz is reputed to have said, early in the Revolution, that Madero had a tiger by the tail (Johnson 132). The same statement might be made with respect to Azuela and the narrative material of *Los de abajo*. Actually, a difference in Azuela's narrative procedure is apparent in *Andrés Pérez, maderista* (1911), a short novel that uses rapidly changing scenes to portray the background of the Madero revolt. In *Los de abajo*, Azuela's "scenes of the Revolution", as his novel is described in its subtitle, create a sense of movement that corresponds to the movement of the troops and also to the change from a static to a dynamic society. Elliptical narration, remarks about the joyful irresponsibility of moving about the countryside, emphasis on the absence of specific purpose, all may be taken as anti-revolutionary, if one thinks about the author's conscious attitude. On the other hand, the novel's deeper communication — what one feels through the experience of it — is a certain inevitability that will not be altered by the defeat of Villa or by anything else. This reading of *Los de abajo* takes into account the contribution of Azuela's narrative strategies to the meaning of the novel, rather than concentrate solely on the events recounted. Traditionally, discussion of Azuela's novel has turned into consideration of whether the author (and incidentally, the novel) was or was not truly revolutionary. One of the book's earliest and most perceptive critics, Eduardo Colín, glimpsed the importance of the author's narrative strategies, even though he was constrained by the canon of his time to emphasize verisimilitude and suggest that the plot should have been more tightly organized. He begins his comments with reference to the sense of urgency created by the elliptical narration (15), and later points out "the impression of primitive and unlimited freedom that moves through these pages. Those people who have everything because of their strength; who march, who come from who knows where and keep on aimlessly, masters of the valleys, the hills, 'as far as your eye can see', this is another of the work's broad implications" (16). Colín also notes specifically the separation of text from author as far as ideology is concerned, emphasizing the point typographically:

...Demetrio Macías, the hero of the novel, strongly delineated at the end, and lying in ambush on a mountain cliff, aiming his rifle unceasingly, always... For how long? This is the main idea of the book (although stated unintentionally) (16).

It is interesting that Colín, writing in 1925 (the year of the "discovery" of *Los de abajo* by Francisco Monterde), saw that the nucleus of the novel's meaning was stated unintentionally.

The effect of a narrative, with respect to its innovative (revolutionary) quality, is not necessarily related to the author's ideology or attitude. It makes perfectly good sense to regard Mariano Azuela as conservative (or as liberal, in the nineteenth-century sense) and still find signs of social rupture in his novels. This disparity has not always been recognized, but literary analysts seem more and more inclined to accept the idea, especially under the persuasiveness of studies like Arturo Arias' on *Hombres de maíz*, by Miguel Angel Asturias. He shows that the ideology of the text is the result of the predominant ideology of a time and place coinciding with and passing through the ideological repertory of an author who is, of course, affected by all aspects of the context in which he lives. Arias is especially interested in analyzing language. That procedure is indeed important, but other narrative strategies also affect the meaning of the work. No doubt Azuela had many reservations about the Revolution, but *Los de abajo* is not a simple reflection of his ideas.

Some of the *ateneístas* were even less enthusiastic than Azuela, with respect to the Revolution; the intellectual revolution does not need arms any more than the armed revolution needs intellect. The two phenomena complement each other, but the relationship is not always apparent to the participants. One would hardly expect Amado Nervo to see his work as in any way auguring an armed rebellion. In a letter to Luis Quintanilla y Fortuño (the father of the younger Luis Quintanilla, one of the *estridentistas*), dated March 7, 1913, Nervo refers, with a feeling of relief, to the imposition of Victoriano Huerta, suggesting that "we all" had been looking for an iron hand to put an end to the chaos that had existed since 1910 (86).

By 1923, the promotion of innovative fiction had become sufficiently strong to make Azuela aware of the strategies he was using. In that year, he published *La malhora*, the first of three novels that are generally considered more innovative than the rest of his work. Actually, it is not spectacularly different. The handling of narrative voice is probably a bit more intricate, and more is left to the reader's imagination, or better, to the reader's ingenuity, since the narrative does not supply all the information one might desire. We note here, again, the quality of incompleteness. It is also significant that Azuela is participating in that search for a suitable direction that characterized the post-Revolutionary years.

In politics, the uncertain, troubled search for a sure way toward the nation's destiny was exemplified in startling, violent assassinations: Zapata in 1919, Carranza in 1920, Villa in 1923, to mention only the names of the most famous. Surely the quest for personal power had much to do with the conflicts that characterize this period; however, another persistent factor was nationalism in its various manifestations, as foreseen in the Ateneo and then in the work of the *colonialistas*. The opposition nationalism-versus-cosmopolitanism at times became nativism-versus-cosmopolitanism; within the concept of nationalism, one observes an opposition between Hispanic tradition and *indigenismo*; the opposition tradition-versus-innovation (change) may substitute *indigenismo* or cosmopolitanism for "innovation", depending on the different shades of meaning granted to the various terms. Hence, the absence of a clearly defined opposition, in politics and in literature.

The period called the "good years" by Cosío Villegas correspond roughly to the presidency of Alvaro Obregón. They were good, not only because of the national sense of accomplishment that Cosío Villegas describes, but also for a sense of confidence created by

Obregón. He seems to have been unpretentious, capable of sympathy for the common people but always with a sense of how much power to retain. He chose José Vasconcelos as his Minister of Education and, although he took a somewhat skeptical view of Vasconcelos' promotion of the classics, he recognized this revolutionary intellectual's importance to the nation (Strode, p.266-268). The work of the Ateneo, some years earlier, indicated that such a convenience (that is, political recognition of the intellectual's role) would have to be reached; the *colonialistas* certainly indicated that any inwardness on the part of Mexico would recognize its Hispanic heritage.

Insofar as it is possible to divide and define the several literary enterprises in Mexico during the nineteen-twenties, the *colonialistas* were followed by the *estridentistas*, a group that adamantly stood for change in artistic expression, though their social position seems rather comfortably bourgeois, in contrast to their radical pronouncements. Naturally, there is a certain overlapping of movements. The *colonialista* movement was effectively ended by 1926; Arqueles Vela, one of the *estridentistas*, published *La señorita Etc.* in 1921, though the movement cannot satisfactorily be dated before the mid-twenties, when its magazines, *Irradiador* and *Horizonte*, were published. If the *colonialistas* presage the conservative turn taken by the Calles government, the radicalism of the *estridentistas* looks forward to a turn to the left in the government of Cárdenas.

Definition of *estridentismo* is not easy. The name in itself is significant. Beyond that, its members referred to Mexico's social problems more than other innovative writers -- e.g., the *colonialistas* or the *Contemporáneos* group. One of the group, Germán List Arzubide, in his account of the movement, says that it tells "the story of the only revolutionary-social-literary movement in Mexico" (List Arzubide, "Colofón"). The colophon itself indicates the heterodoxy of the group: not only does it comment on the nature of the book, it comments on the date of publication, and it is preceded by a page bearing only the word "Colofón", in large, bold-face type, as if it were announcing an important section of the text. Like some European vanguardist publications of the same period, List Arzubide's book is highly visual, and verbal descriptions of it hardly suffice. Among other things (a paste-in of a mask made by the sculptor, Germán Cueto, a "pentagramatic poem" by Pedro Echeverría, a photograph of telephone wires by Tina Modotti, for example), it contains reproductions of the art of Alva de la Canal, the principal visual artist of the movement. His paintings and woodblocks show a strong Cubist influence. It is noteworthy, in this connection, the Picón-Garfield and Schulman refer to the *estridentistas'* "zeal for Cubist representation" (158). If we add to this interest a certain amount of futurism, we have a reasonably adequate idea of the group's canon. It would be appropriate to mention a considerable quantity of sheer youthful exuberance.

While Cubism certainly reached Mexico via the artists of the period who studied in Paris, it did not exclude nationalism. Diego Rivera, while still in Paris and during his Cubist phase, used Mexican subject matter (Arquin 80). No doubt the motives behind this preference were complex, but we may be sure that among them were the satisfaction provided by a different line and the freedom afforded by polyfaceted representation. It may seem a bit forced to project a Cubist-like narrative that is analogous to Cubist painting, but that is surely what interested the *estridentistas* in the nineteen-twenties, and it is just as surely what appears in later fictions as "simultaneity" (*simultaneismo*), or fragmentation, or multiple point-of-view, or antichronology, or any combination of these variously named phenomena.

If Alva de la Canal may be considered the *estridentistas'* semi-official artist, Arqueles Vela occupies the same position in prose fiction. His major work, a short novel called *El Café de Nadie* (Nobody's Cafe), was published in 1926. The title is an important element in the novel because the *estridentista* group used to refer to their favorite meeting place, a cafe in Colonia Roma, as the "Café de Nadie." It is, to a considerable extent, a narrative written for an "in group", an interpretation of the significance of this place to the people who made it their unofficial headquarters. Luis Mario Schneider names more than a dozen writers, painters, and musicians who frequented the Café de Nadie (18). Vela himself gives a more extensive list as part of the narrative (36-7). The degrcc of diffcrencc from the establishment must have varied considerably among the individual members of the group; for example, the aggressive, anti-tradition provocation by Manuel Maples Arce seems far removed from the metaphysical system of metaphors employed by Arqueles Vela in his attempt to achieve *tabula rasa* and then rebuild.

Vela's narrator tells us, at the very beginning, that the threshold of the cafe is "like the last stairstep of reality," by means of which you "enter the subway (he uses the English word) of dreams, of ideation" (11). The following imagery suggests a stasis, a synchronic circumstance in which various observed phenomena contribute to the same meaning — or perhaps better, the same sensation. Material objects exist in some half recognized state that is removed from reality and is still not quite unreal. The people in the novel experience this strange state; readers see the characters in exactly the same way — that is, the characters themselves are somewhere between real and unreal. They are especially notable for the quality of "decharacterization" that Gustavo Pérez Firmat sees in the vanguardist novel. Mabelina, the center of narrative attention, feels her spirit broken and her body transmigrated "to all the shadows where it contemplated itself and abstracted itself, recognizing its immoderate movements that were tapestrying the room with decorations of dreams" (23). Mabelina, like others in the narrative, is in a constant state of change and has finally become a sketch (the English word is used again) of herself. "After being all women, now she was nobody" (38). Of course, this condition makes her the ideal patron of Nobody's Cafe.

Vela's images use material objects to communicate the mood of a person or the atmosphere of a place, and sometimes they are startlingly unpoetic. On restraining an impulse to express her love by kissing a man, Mabelina remains "still, frightened, as if in the electric chair of love" (22). This image recalls many instances in which the *estridentistas* used objects of modern technology as artistic devices. One feels that they were forcing the issue of modernness, via such imagery and also via other deviations from customary narrative strategies. Vela, for example, used typographic effects that make one think of concretist poetry, mentioned jazz, used English words, produced a schematic *récit* that requires readers to compensate, extraordinarily, for the unstated.

The concern for social protest that may be associated with some *estridentista* work is not apparent in *El Café de Nadie*. However, readers of the novel necessarily sense the implied author's impatience with the status quo, the need to join the twentieth century, to question ordinary concepts of reality, and to do great things. It is highly significant — however strange the association — that the same year, 1926, saw the publication of Vela's novel and the outbreak of the *cristero* rebellions, an expression of traditionalist extremism. President Calles' government was virtually forced, by a complicated series of maneuvers on the part of the clergy, to take a strong anti-clerical position, enforcing the provisions of the constitution that were designed to limit the political power of the church — that is, the influence of the church on its communicants, in matters other than faith and worship (Cumberland, 276-281).

The government's radical anti-clerical position was clearly against tradition, though the Calles government could not be described generally in those terms. It was an intensely political regime, inclined to take the convenient road, and in so doing, had acquired a certain populist character through association with labor and agrarian unions. It may seem ironic, from a certain point of view, that the *cristero* movement, a traditionalist undertaking, was supported by the peasant population, since one tends to associate traditionalism with social elitism. However, the true nature of the conflict is deeply rooted in Mexican history, and transcends social and economic class lines; it amounts to a struggle between the civil government and the ecclesiastical authority for control of the populace. In other words, what authority do the people accept? The nature of the *cristero* conflict — that is, its combination of traditionalism and peasant support — further complicates the polarity, or polarities, of the era.

To the radical change called for by Arqueles Vela's brand of *estridentismo*, Xavier Icaza added a specific social problem, including concern for the rural poor, in *Panchito Chapopote* (1928). The protagonist, Panchito, becomes wealthy when oil is found on his property. The petroleum controversy goes back to the Díaz regime when foreign interests, mainly British and American, virtually took control of the industry in Mexico. By 1925, worker unrest caused President Calles to threaten the foreign entrepreneurs with a modification of their status. The legal basis behind the Mexican position was the principle of subsoil rights belonging to the nation, propounded in the eighteenth century by Charles III of Spain, and stated also in the constitution of 1917. The consequent maneuvering went on until President Cárdenas expropriated the petroleum properties in 1938.

Icaza's novel looks back in time to project the competition between the United States and Great Britain for Panchito's property. They reach a compromise that enriches Panchito, but hardly in proportion to what the two political/economic powers have gained. At the point in the narrative when the compromise is reached, the representatives of the two nations are magically transformed into Uncle Sam and John Bull as part of a phantasmagoric bi-national victory pageant. The narrative then returns to the narrator's present, and to Panchito. We find much American influence in the locale: asphalt highway, expensive but bad hotels, American cuisine ("Lonches. Quick lonch. Free Lonch. Banana lonch." 64), trucks, business men from everywhere.

Attention continues to be focused on Panchito until the events become so much more important than Panchito that the Author enters the narrative to tell his protagonist that he is no longer needed (76-77). Over Panchito's protests, the Author arranges his demise. This procedure is only one of many modernist aspects of the novel. Icaza defies every custom of genre. Often the narrative resembles the text of a play, composed of dialogue and stage directions. But it is not consistently so. There is also descriptive narration, in a staccato style. Folk songs serve as narrative devices, and radio loudspeakers facilitate long distance communication.

Icaza's novel is clearly innovative in narrative strategy. Its use of modern technology and its insistence on brevity are similar of *estridentista* works in general. The abruptness of his expression is like Maples Arce's iconoclasm: "the appropriate strategy was fast action and total subversion" (Schneider, 11). Icaza himself, in a 1934 address, announced that art for art's sake was no longer a viable possibility, that the world needed changing, and intellectuals were called upon to do it. "Thus is born social, vanguardist art" (38). He advises against the trappings of realism and proposes a more essential expression that will take into account the folkloric and will be, above all, brief (44). This statement of principle bears some consideration with respect to the modernist tendency of the *estridentistas*, since the combination of popular culture and high culture is considered by some to be a characteristic of post-modernism, e.g., the definition of Néstor García Canclini. However, there seems to be a difference between two cases, one in which popular culture is incorporated into high culture in such a way that the end result is really high culture, and a different case in which the joining of high and low produces a result that cannot be defined as either high or low. It is a fair assumption that Icaza, in *Panchito Chapopote*, was thinking of the second case, but the novel did not achieve that comprehensive range. This fact does not diminish to even the slightest degree the *estridentistas'* attack on what they considered elitist in art. One of the group's most vehement members, Manuel Maples Arce, signed a *manifiesto* of protest when the Palacio de Bellas Artes was opened in 1934. Francisco Reyes Palma, writing about the less than peaceful beginnings of the great theatre, states that downtown Mexico City was papered with copies of the document (34). Of course, by that time, Mexico was on the verge of the socialistically oriented Cárdenas regime, a change which had already been forecast by the novel through its preoccupation with the nation's social problems.

Icaza's combination of innovative technique and social protest may be seen as a link between vanguardist narrative and the socially oriented novels of the nineteen-thirties and nineteen-forties; it may also be seen as an anticipation of a more sophisticated combination of narrative experimentation and national themes found a bit later in Revueltas, Yañez, and Rulfo. Relating *Panchito Chapopote* to the realm of politics, the novel seems to reflect, thematically, the urgency faced by the Calles government in 1925 and to anticipate, through the diminution of Panchito, an even more dramatic decision by Cárdenas. Its narrative strategies certainly correspond to the attempt, by many different forces, to pull (or perhaps "explode" might be better in the case of the *estridentistas*) Mexico into the modern world.

Politics between the end of the Calles presidency, in 1928, and the inauguration of Cárdenas, in 1934, were remarkably confused. It was a period dominated by Calles, but that statement alone is the well known tip of the iceberg. Toward the end of Calles' term, the ruling party effected a constitutional change that would lengthen the presidential term to six years and also permit the reelection to President Obregón. This procedure was not universally approved, for some feared the possibility of an indefinite rotation of Calles and Obregón (Parkes, 387). One of the leaders who objected, General Francisco Serrano, was assassinated, and following the election, so was President-elect Obregón. The Congress, inspired by Calles, named Emilio Portes Gil to serve as president for one year. In 1929, Pascual Ortiz Rubio, another Calles choice, was elected with such a vast majority over his opponent, José Vasconcelos, that the numbers are ludicrous to the point of being incredible. In the fall of 1932, Portes Gil displeased his political mentor and was summarily sent to the United States for a rest. Calles then instructed Congress to name Abelardo Rodríguez, who filled the remainder of what would have been Obregón's second term.

The period between 1928 and 1934 is a succinct example of the political quest (the search for a suitable way) that characterized Mexican politics from the Revolution to the presidency of Cárdenas. The literary scene was similarly confused. A remnant of *colonialista* narrative remained; *estridentismo* was still a force. And, almost ironically, during this same period, Mexico's most famous literary magazine, *Contemporáneos*, flourished. These different groups (one can hardly call them "literary movements") are aspects of a common desire to effect change. Even the *colonialistas*, who based their works on tradition, revealed, through their narrative strategies and the way they perceived the past, that they too were searching for a modern identity. The confusion naturally caused by the differences among these groups was exacerbated by an intensifying inclination to deal with Mexican society and its problems. Each group participated in this process according to its own perception of what the process should be. One should also note that the concern for national problems, as a growing concern in the society, includes the tendency toward a more socialistic political structure, with the accompanying discussions about social justice, morality, freedom, etc.

The censorship of Rubén Salazar Mallén's *Cariatide*, in 1932, helps provide some specific sense of this period of confusion. Sections of this novel were published in the magazine *Examen*, edited by Jorge Cuesta, a member of the *Contemporáneos* group. An outraged press, supposedly representing a public whose good taste had been offended by the novel's "dirty" language, led to charges being brought against the novelist and the editor. They were exonerated by the court, on the grounds that the words in themselves were neither moral nor immoral, but the episode endures as a kind of witness to its time.

The *Cariátide* affair has not been evaluated as fully as one might like, because the author, presumably in disgust and anger, burned most of the manuscript. However, Edward J. Mullen, in an analysis of the available information, notes more than one reason for the reaction against the novel (1981, 63). He points out that the objection raised by *El Machete*, the organ of the Communist party in Mexico, is based on the novel's negative image of the party, while those of *Excelsior* are based on a definition of good taste, and also seem inspired by the newspaper's dislike of the *Contemporáneos* group. The latter is hardly surprising, since the group was frequently attacked for a variety of reasons, ranging from xenomania to homosexuality (Brushwood, 1964). The matter of sexual preference was more concerned with what might be call "feminization" of art than with the nature of personal relationships. The transition toward concern for national problems seemed to call for a stronger (read "macho") statement, well removed from the hyperartistic work of the *Contemporáneos* group.

The issue of poor taste, translated into a question of morality, may also have contributed to the reaction of *El Machete*. A rather straitlaced attitude toward certain kinds of behavior is quite apparent in leftist literature. In the magazine *Crisol*, which was in many respects an opposite to *Contemporáneos*, the eminent Guatemalan writer, Rafael Arévalo Martínez, published a poem warning the common man of three preeminent dangers: malaria, bad women, and alcohol. This piece of doggerel appeared in the same issue with an essay by another poet, Carlos Gutiérrez Cruz, in which he condemns all literature that is not accessible to, and helpful to, the working class. The highly stylized narrative of Salazar Mallén obviously was not written for the common man, and what is more important, it could have been considered immoral and dangerous.

In connection with the transition from vanguardism to a more socially oriented novel, one should note that Salazar Mallén had published stories in *Contemporáneos*, in which he used an elliptical narrative procedure, challenging the reader to fill in information that would complete the *histoire*; he also cultivated the suggestively intimate though elusive characterization so common among the vanguardists. Mullen points out that *Cariátide* represents a "fairly clear break" with the *Contemporáneos* group (1981, 60). The author maintains a rather unorthodox narrative procedure, but he is clearly referring to a specifically Mexican circumstance, probably a recent occurrence in Mexico City, and he employs what is commonly referred to as "street language" (Mullen 1981, 61-62). One notes the combination of certain vanguardist tendencies with greater attention to the Mexican circumstance.

Significantly, the *Cariátide* affair occurred one year after the demise of the magazine *Contemporáneos*, an important association in observing the transition form vanguardism to committed literature. Meanwhile, the magazine had contributed to forming a basis for Mexican literature that would never be destroyed, no matter what nuances of literary interest might appear. *Contemporáneos* and several writers closely associated with it have become the standard example of vanguardist literature in Mexico. A broad definition of vanguardism would include *estridentismo* and some other writers like Julio Torri and Efrén Hernández, but there is a clear preference, among literary specialists, for concentrating on *Contemporaneos*. Its characterizing quality might be described, superficially, as "polished sophistication," in contrast to the explosive, brave-new-world posture of the *estridentistas*. The intent of its editors and collaborators was to make a modern magazine, like the *Nouvelle Revue Francaise* or the *Revista de Occidente*. Its internationalist outlook evoked much criticism of the magazine and of its contributors by more nationalistically oriented writers, especially in *Crisol*. This discrepancy was never as great in actuality as it was in discussion, or in the subsequently developed perception of the polemic.

Contemporáneos paid a great deal of attention to Mexican literature, art and music, even to a consideration of the Mexican essence, through the work of Samuel Ramos. However, it was not militantly nationalistic; rather, it seems to have looked for the position of Mexican culture in a larger, universal context. Edward J. Mullen notes the European influence on Ramos and on other Mexican essayists, and also the similarities between *Contemporáneos* and other vanguardist magazines (1972, 29-42). The point to be emphasized here is that these intellectuals were not unpatriotic. Far from ignoring Mexican reality, they intended to establish Mexico's identity in the context of contemporary European Culture. This attitude would not see the nationalism/cosmopolitanism controversy as fundamental; rather, it points up the dichotomy between being modern and being out-of-date. A good example of this position is Jaime Torres Bodet's commentary on the poetry of Ramón López Velarde, in which the critic emphasizes the poet's growth outward from a very limited regional referent to an increasingly larger context, but without ever losing the sense of regional identity (Nos. 28-29, pp. 111-135). It is also significant, in this connection, that the editors chose to publish excerpts from Mariano Azuela's *La luciérnaga* (No. 3, pp. 235-252, No. 23, pp.

20-33) and *La malhora* (Nos. 30-31, pp. 193-216, No. 32, pp. 42-70), two of the author's most innovative novels, though both works are eminently Mexican in theme.

Whatever the true inclination of *Contemporáneos*, it was involved in the cosmopolitanism/nationalism dispute on two different levels. In the first place, as a representative of cosmopolitanism, it was defended or attacked because of that position. On another level, the magazine involved itself, internally, in the consideration of how the reality of being Mexican was related to the position of Mexico in an international context. The work of Carlos Mérida, probably the painter most closely related to the review, shows the same concern, in a non-literary medium.

As has traditionally been the case in studying vanguardism, the poetry of the "Contemporáneos group" has received much more attention than the prose fiction. Recently, Gustavo Pérez Firmat's *Idle Fictions* has been helpful in filling this void by referring to the novels of Torres Bodet, Gilberto Owen, Xavier Villaurrutia, and a *vanguardista* not closely associated with *Contemporáneos*, José Martínez Sotomayor. To these names, one might well add Salvador Novo and Efrén Hernández. The common denominator among their narratives is their "pneumatic" quality, to use the terminology of Pérez Firmat. Clear yet succinct definition of this kind of fiction is not possible, but its quality may be suggested by saying that it refers to an evanescent reality. Characters tend to fade; figuratively speaking, portraits become silhouettes. It is interesting, in this connection, that Merlin H. Forster, writing of the two women in *Margarita de Niebla* (1927), refers to their ambiguousness and silences [this information taken from a copy of the manuscript which was later published in *La Palabra y el Hombre*]. Locale tends to be specified vaguely; even the action (what little there is) tends to be otherworldly, not representative of ordinary life, but interpretative in such a way that aspects of ordinary life are recognizable in ethereal form. Pérez Firmat and Forster explain the relationship between the writers mentioned above and the Spanish novelist, Benjamín Jarnés (incidentally, represented in *Contemporáneos*), and also their similarity to Jean Giraudoux.

Some of these qualities are present in *El Café de Nadie*, but Vela's novel is more shocking linguistically, less "lyrical" than the narratives analyzed by Pérez Firmat. It is important to surround "lyrical" with quotation marks because it is not quite accurate to say that such novels are poetic, as Pérez Firmat shows most convincingly in his analysis of Torres Bodet's *Margarita de niebla*, 1927 (Pérez F., 81-95). Although it is true that one reads *Margarita de niebla* closely, and with the expectation of figurative language, as in reading poetry, the experience is somewhat different.

Pérez Firmat shows that there is a plain and simple love story that exists somewhere behind or beneath the narrative that we read, but such a love story is not what we experience. Rather, we experience the effort to characterize Margarita. Her suitor, Borja, is the narrator, and one might reasonably expect a psychological novel of character. But Borja seems never to capture the essence, never to communicate clearly the reality of Margarita. To quote Pérez Firmat, ". . . though *Margarita de niebla* cannot be read fruitfully as a novel of character, it can be regarded as a novel *about* character, as an inquiry into the question of characterization in fiction" (83). He goes on to point out that Torres Bodet's novel belongs to a long tradition of fictions that project a well rounded character, but function as a critique of that tradition. This quality clearly defines the work as a modernist novel. For the average reader who probably does not think about such matters, *Margarita de niebla* provides more ambience than characterization. It exudes the feeling of the upper-middle-class environment in the nineteen-twenties. It is something like a novel of manners, yet never becomes exactly that, because it is not a critique of manners. It is all too vague, too distant and, therefore, is a kind of critique of the novel of manners, just as it is a critique of traditional characterization.

Similarly modern qualities are found in Gilberto Owen's *Novela como nube* (1928), José Martínez Sotomayor's *La rueca de aire* (1930), and other vanguardist novels. The description of them as "modern" is based on both technique and thematic material. The narrative strategy depends largely on focalization that produces an intensely subjective view of persons and places. This view may or may not be that of the person who narrates; in either case it is subjective to the point of subverting both character and story line. In some cases, and especially in the case of Owen, figurative diction increases the sense of intangibleness. These techniques become related to theme through references to classical mythology and literary figures, as well as to popular culture and mechanical devices of the nineteen-twenties, e.g. Buster Keaton, automobiles, electric signs. The important point is that these references are intercalated in such a way that no type has priority over another. The effect created by this combination of technique and theme is like seeing the world of F. Scott Fitzgerald through a theatrical scrim.

Length of the narrative is of little importance. Some of the novels are quite short, and Efrén Hernández's famous short stories, "Tachas" (1928) and "El señor de palo" (1932), are clearly in the same vein. "Tachas" could well be considered, along with *Margarita de niebla*, as a critique of traditional characterization. "El señor de palo" is a critique of the whole process of narration; it is a narrative that really is *about* narrating, although, on one level, it may be said to be about a love affair and a jealous husband (a story that is not really told).

These pyrotechnics of the imagination are most appealing to readers who are actively involved in some process of artistic creativity, or readers who are stimulated intellectually by a challenge to reality and to tradition. Occasional allusions to things Mexican are so incidental they do little or nothing to make the fiction seem more representational (of Mexican social reality). To this extent, vanguardist fiction stands guilty of the elitism and xenomania of which it was accused. On the other hand, it seems reasonable to see it as one manifestation of the post-World War I (and in Mexico, post-Revolution) ebullience and confidence that encouraged innovation and the desire to be modern.

Pérez Firmat ponders the slight endurance of the vanguardist novel (21, and elsewhere). Considering this kind of fiction in connection with the real world and those events that we commonly take to be the facts of history, it is reasonable to think that a creation which is, in some sense, a negation of reality, must inevitably exist rather tenuously within its context. In the nineteen-thirties, an accumulation of social concerns would not encourage the writing of such fictions.

Specifically in Mexico, one can see that, from the early nineteen-thirties, novels concerned with typically Mexican affairs — the Revolution and its consequences — begin to establish their dominance over more cosmopolitan fiction. One should not assume that this "Mexicanist" trend is entirely without innovation in narrative procedure; an examination of novels by Gregorio López y Fuentes, for example, would prove otherwise. The great difference is that Mexican themes gradually become pervasive and, although innovative techniques are sometimes used, innovation is not primary. There is certainly no sense of evanescent reality in them. With regard to this difference, Pérez Firmat notes that Torres Bodet, the most prolific of the vanguardist novelists, wrote novels with a firmer hold on their subjects, as his career moved on (Pérez F., 95). There is no way of proving that this change in Torres Bodet is related to the growing emphasis, in fiction, on typically Mexican subjects, but it may be that both phenomena are expressions of a tendency to examine specific problems of society, a need that could not be entirely satisfied by any of the novelistic innovations of the nineteen-twenties. One can argue that Torres Bodet's novels always dealt with Mexican social reality, as in the reflection of the cosmopolitanism/nationalism controversy in the opposing characterizations of Margarita and Paloma.

The beginning of the Lázaro Cárdenas presidency, in 1934, is highly significant in this connection. It may be regarded as having indicated, for however brief a time, a specific course for the nation. Even a casual look into the future reveals the transitoriness of this choice, but such a view does not alter its basic nature. It marked a clear path after a period of searching, of experimentation, of indeterminacy. In a way, this presidency effected an implementation of the post-Revolutionary euphoria that Cosío Villegas called "the good years" of the Revolution. Programs of land reform were put into effect, the railroads were nationalized and turned over to the

workers, public education was made socialist, the petroleum industry was expropriated. All these programs may be described as nationalistic, directly concerned with specifically Mexican circumstances. But at the same time, certain events outside Mexico would
inevitably distract the nation from its inward contemplation. Of extraordinary importance, in this regard, was the arrival of refugees
from the Spanish Civil War. And near the end of his administration, President Cárdenas felt compelled to protest Germany's invasion of Belgium, Holland, and Luxemburg.

At about the time President Cárdenas took office, the *period* of
vanguardist innovation had ended. Specific thematic material had
become more prominent that suggestive ambience, simple narration was favored over experimentation, nationalism predominated,
cosmopolitanism declined. It is necessary to state these facts in
terms of a *period*, because the kinds of fiction written during the
nineteen-twenties and early nineteen-thirties (they may be identified collectively as innovative/cosmopolitan) did not simply disappear. Such novels continued to occupy a place, albeit less prominent, in the literary spectrum. Torres Bodet, in *Primero de enero*
(1935) and *Sombras* (1937), continued the line, though with some
modifications, as noted by Pérez Firmat. The line was strength-
ened by others, among them Salazar Mallén and Eduardo Luquín.
But the dominant fiction corresponded to the politics of the time.
In the early nineteen-thirties, the search for an appropriate kind of
fiction was joined by the inwardly oriented nationalistic concern.
The latter became dominant at about the time Cárdenas became
president.

As was the case with politics, this inwardness would be transitory.
Just as it became necessary, in the nineteen-forties, for the Mexican government to recognize its place in an international context,
so also the novelists found a way to combine national identity and
cosmopolitanism. They developed the combination of modern narrative strategies and national themes, a combination that is especially apparent in well-known novels by José Revueltas, Agustín
Yañez, and Juan Rulfo. This new novel reaffirms the vanguardist
enterprise and incorporates the national interest. In contrast to

the volatile nineteen-twenties and early nineteen-thirties, when innovation in narrative seemed sometimes to anticipate political
change, both novel and politics, in the later nineteen-thirties, seem
more stable, more coordinated, and both are more representational
(that is, closer to commonly perceived reality). The subsequent
move toward internationalism was gradual, the novel using modern
techniques to interpret its context, the political structure adjusting
national policy to the exigencies of its international commitment.
This process is the story of innovation from the middle of the nineteen-forties until the middle of the nineteen-sixties, when innovation in the novel again becomes dramatically apparent.

Chapter 2

The International Context of Nationalism (1942-1958)

The vertiginous rate of change during the nineteen-twenties and early nineteen-thirties was not equalled until dissatisfaction with the *status quo* was expressed in several different ways during the nineteen-sixties. Narrative innovations by *colonialistas*, *estridentistas*, and the *Contemporáneos* group seem almost frenetic when contrasted with literary strategies used during the years immediately following. So also in the political realm; while change is apparent during the quarter-century following the election of Lázaro Cárdenas, the process seems more gradual.

The internalized, national focus of the Cárdenas government corresponds to a trend observable in the novel since 1931. That year is remarkable for the emphasis placed by novelists on the Revolution. This material had already been used sparingly, but it seems that, by 1931, the fact of the Revolution had reached a certain maturity, within the national consciousness, that required literary expression. It would be absurd, of course, to suppose that all novels of the Revolution employ the same narrative strategies. Nevertheless, as a thematic subgenre, they did not emphasize innovation; rather, they suggest a strong desire to tell how it was, in a straightforward way. This quality has often prompted the use of *relato* (tale) as an identifier of the type. The no-nonsense storytelling accords well with the populist character of the approaching Cárdenas presidency.

Just as the Revolution is understood in two senses (the military phase, and the more extensive period of social adjustment following the armed conflict), so the novel deals not only with the fight-but also with the social issues that came into prominence as a result of the struggle. The position of the indigenous peoples in the national culture was naturally an important issue. The owner-ship of land, a corollary problem, also became subject matter for novelists. And there was some treatment of the urban poor, but it is important to remember that, in the nineteen-thirties, industrialization in Mexico had not progressed far, so urban problems seem less important, as we look back on the period, than rural ones.

The circumstances described and interpreted in narrative fiction were precisely those portrayed by the great muralists. They were, in fact, the problems for which the Cárdenas government proposed ameliorative programs. This attention to the national situation worked at cross-purposes to the cosmopolitan inclination of vanguardist fiction. However, the latter influence did not disappear. In a position of apparently secondary importance, it persisted as a doorway through which novelists could return to more inventive narration.

It is no exaggeration to say that the Cárdenas government identified a road — or procedure — for the nation, and because this road was well defined, the impulse to experiment diminished. In fact, the impulse became subdued in the novel before the Cárdenas government stabilized the political situation. With regard to President Cárdenas' policies, one should never forget that they represented one path for the nation, not the only path. Twelve years after the Cárdenas regime began, Miguel Alemán became president and initiated an entirely different program. In a few inadequate words, one can say that the Cárdenas plan intended to change the economic structure of the nation along socialist lines; the Alemán program was industrialization and capital expansion that presumably would benefit all sectors of society. For obvious reasons, the *alemanista* approach placed Mexico more directly in contact with the developed nations, so promoting the search for a Mexican identity within a larger context. It is worth noting, in this connection, that John Johnson, in his study of the "urban middle sectors," points out that this sector of society struggled through the period of radical agrarianism and returned to prominence in the nineteen-forties (128 ff.).

Even before the end of his administration, Cárdenas' attention was externalized, forcibly, by the Spanish Civil War and by Fascist aggression in Europe. His successor, Manuel Avila Camacho, presided over the country from 1940 to 1946, when World War II practically demanded Mexico's externalization. During these years, change in Mexico was ordained fully as much by external circumstances as by internal policy. This fact is emphasized by the position of Avila Camacho between two intensely persistent political figures, Cárdenas and Alemán, who held strongly opposing views. In other words, so far as policy was concerned, the Avila Camacho presidency was a period of little internally motivated innovation, between two very active administrations (Basañez, 61-62). During those years of relative calm, a change toward internationalism began in the novel, possibly by conscious intent on the part of the writers.

Technical innovation was the key in this new movement in prose fiction. Far from cultivating an interest in cosmopolitan subject matter, the writers used clearly identifiable Mexican material, transforming it, by different narrative strategies, so that regionalistic material transcended the limitations normally exercised by the nature of regionalism. This movement was more gradual, though no less radical, than the innovations of the nineteen-twenties and early nineteen-thirties. The transformation of national themes, the cosmopolitanization of regionalism (one begs readers to accept his seeming paradox), beginning in the nineteen-forties and continuing in the following decade, anticipated the Alemán government's projection of Mexico into the international scene. One may ask whether or not the literary enterprise and the political one were equally successful.

In the novel, the aspects of this gradual change may be seen most clearly by reference to four well known novels: *El luto humano* (1943), by José Revueltas, *Al filo del agua* (1947), by Agustín Yáñez, *Pedro Páramo* (1955), by Juan Rulfo, and *La región más transparente* (1958), by Carlos Fuentes. Since the merging of national and international interests takes place with increasing intensity during the period 1942-1958, it is of some importance to note that *El luto humano* was published during the first half of the Avila Camacho presidency, *Al filo del agua* very early in the Alemán administration, and the other two during the term of Alemán's successor, Adolfo Ruiz Cortines. The character-istics of these novels are corroborated in several ways by others, written during the same period, that have been relegated to a posi-tion of secondary importance, though not for any reason that diminishes their relevance to the present study.

The quality of transcendent regionalism, found in the novels of this period, is associated with the phenomenon generally referred to as the "new novel" in Latin America. One of the earliest candi-dates for this classification in Mexico is *El luto humano*, a novel in which Revueltas portrays a tiny community of working people who face death and natural disaster as factors added to the ever present frustration of unsatisfactory personal relationships. Their anguish, closely akin to existentialism, is a cosmopolitan condition not found in earlier novels about the Mexican working class. Three couples, all of them mismatched, are trapped by the storm, at a pathetic wake for the dead child of Ursulo and Cecilia: "Ursulo turned to look at his wife, with intense anger because she was with Calixto. Now he understood vaguely the hazy relationships that arise be-tween love and death, or between hate and death. It was necessary for Chonita to die so all this might happen. So Cecilia, like a black, desperate animal, would turn against him. Nevertheless, he didn't dare do anything, although the brightness of his eyes emitted a dry blood, without relief" (43). This passage illustrates the author's way of describing a character's feelings with an intensity of lan-guage that some readers find exaggeratedly emotional. Fortu-nately, in some cases, he chooses to "show" rather than "tell".

As the same scene develops, attention shifts to "La Calixta," the wife of Calixto. Tension grows in the room until, at one point, Ur-sulo commands, "Nobody gets out of here" (44). La Calixta chal-lenges him with a look and a "Nobody?", after which she throws her weight against the door and disappears into the storm. The self-identification accomplished through this act becomes clearer, much later in the novel, when a retrospective passage tells how the relationship of this couple began. The woman had asked Calixto to take her with him because she believed he would beat her less than the man with whom she had been living (104). It is important to note, however, that she never acquired an identity, was never known as anything but "La Calixta" (Calixto's woman).

The abrogation of cause/effect relationship in these passages is extremely interesting. An immediate cause (tension and awareness of unsatisfactory relationships) is apparent before effect (La Calixta's self-determining act), but the more distant cause does not become apparent until much later in the narrative. Obviously, this novel is more than a denunciation of poverty, no matter how much one may deplore the living conditions of the characters. These conditions, which we may accept as an authentic Mexican circumstance, are presented in an intellectual context — one might think of it as a philosophical code — that is generally present, during the nineteen-forties, in international fiction. The social context of *El luto humano* corresponds to the internal focus of the Cárdenas era. But an international "code" makes its presence felt, perhaps inevitably, as in the politics of the Avila Camacho years. Certainly it forecasts the purposeful internationalism of Alemán and beyond.

The nationalist/internationalist contrast was given a special twist, in the nineteen-forties, by a particularly American (that is, Western Hemisphere) interest. This preference was different from the *novomundismo* of the early twentieth century, which extolled the geographic and demographic peculiarities of the hemisphere. The nineteen-forties phenomenon was more like cultural isolationism. In Mexico, it may well have had its beginning in the arrival of refugees from the Spanish Civil War, and it may have been intensified by the inclination to stay out of World War II, but the manifestation was inter-American, not uni-nationalistic. Boyd G. Carter points out that the magazine *Cuadernos Americanos*, one of the most important Spanish-language magazines of the century, was founded in 1942 by a group of Mexicans and Spaniards, not primarily to promote literature, but to deal with American political, social, and economic issues as well (148). *América*, the long-lived magazine renowned for its presentation of famous-writers-to-be (Rulfo, Castellanos, Sabines, Arreola, for example) had already started publication in 1940. But more to the point, here, is the appearance, in 1943, of *El Hijo Pródigo*, a magazine that, according to its founder, Octavio G. Barreda, was intended to operate as a balancing factor to the "continental policy" of *Cuadernos Americanos*, which tended to ignore Europe as a vital force (Barreda, 232). Carter considers *El Hijo Pródigo* a worthy heir to the literary enterprise of *Contemporáneos* (151). So we note, in *El Hijo Pródigo* and *Cuadernos Americanos*, that the nationalist/cosmopolitan polemic had turned in a slightly different direction, but the basic issue was still the relationship with Europe.

Rubén Salazar Mallén's *Páramo* (1944), one of the unsung novels of this period, is of special interest in connection with the *americanista* tendency, because its protagonist is an idealistic professor who would promote his own version of the pan-American dream (not the Pan American Union or the Organization of American States). *Páramo* seems to have been published privately, since no publishing house is mentioned; it was printed in the "Talleres de la Editorial Stylo." The book contains a "Posdata" in which the author states that the novel was to have been published by *El Hijo Pródigo*, but later was rejected because it was considered reactionary (233-4). The "Posdata" accuses the editors of political prejudice and stupidity, even the "talented ones" like Octavio Paz and José Revueltas (234). In view of Barreda's statement about the role of *El Hijo Pródigo* in maintaining awareness of the Western Hemisphere's relationship with Europe, one wonders if the "reactionary" quality referred to in the "Posdata" may not have been the protagonist's *americanista* dream. It is especially interesting that, at the end of *Páramo*, the idealist deplores the disaster at Pearl Harbor and concludes that chaos will ensue.

The course of international events continued to demonstrate the inevitable relationship of Mexico to the rest of the world, and the government declared war on the Axis powers in 1942, the year before *El Hijo Pródigo's* founders reaffirmed the vital importance of

Europe. In the same year, however, President Avila Camacho continued promotion of the nation's internal awareness by convening the living ex-presidents, in a project of national unity. Naturally, in time of war, national unity is an expected condition. On the other hand, the analogous external/internal combination of concern in narrative may not be noticed unless it is pointed out in *El luto humano* and other books of the period.

A second generally ignored novel, *Konco*, by A. Núñez Alonso, published in 1943, adds still another element to the portrait of the period: the presence of a transnational company in Mexico. When this novel was written, foreign investment and industrialization were becoming more important, spurred on by the Second World War. On the other hand, Mexico was only a few years removed from the expropriation of petroleum, and *Konco* anticipated a far more complicated industrial/commercial complex than was the fact at the time it was written. The narrative is not technically innovative. Using basically orthodox chronology, the author interweaves lines of commercial and personal intrigue. Power is an ever present consideration as the principals deal on several different social and moral levels, including contact with a Central American dictator.

These three novels of the early nineteen-forties provide a significant, if somewhat complicated, portrait of the time, with the trend toward internationalism eminently clear. *El luto humano* leaves no doubt about the author's concern for the working class, but it also shows, just as clearly, the presence of a European philosophical influence in the projection of human relationships. *Páramo* is an anguished cry of anti-Europeanism, with defeat of its idea guaranteed by the intradiegetic reference to Pearl Harbor. *Konco* looks forward, quite accurately, to a more complicated industrial/commercial configuration than was the case at the time it was written. In his essay on the plastic arts and politics in Mexico, Reyes Palma states that "Once the euphoria of nationalizations had passed, *cardenismo* flowed along a more conservative course that touched bottom with the regime of his successor, Manuel Avila Camacho" (37). He goes on to explain that the system of socialist education, instituted by the Cárdenas government, was abandoned in favor of a moralizing emphasis on family and patriotism. This change marked the beginning of a decline in the importance of social commitment in the plastic arts, and according to Reyes Palma, some critics have designated the year 1949 as marking the end of social realism (41). He points out that, of course, social realism did not disappear completely and suddenly. This exposition reveals the other side of the coin that shows the trajectory of vanguardism. In the early nineteen-thirties, one can see the increasing predominance of socially committed fiction over vanguardist innovation, so anticipating the policies of the Cárdenas government; in the nineteen-forties, one notes the growing importance of internationalism (with vanguardist characteristics) as social commitment diminished — or perhaps better, was transformed into a more universal expression. However, vanguardism/cosmopolitanism did not disappear completely in the first case, nor did social commitment in the second.

Important as subject matter may be, narrative strategies are equally indicative with respect to the meaning of the novel as an organ of society. Octavio Paz long ago, in 1943, recognized the innovative quality of *El luto humano* (Paz 1984, 141-145). Undoubtedly, Revueltas' manipulation of multiple point-of-view provided a very different vision of the Revolution and its consequences. This procedure indicates, in the first place, a relatively sophisticated awareness of how modern narrative works; relative, that is, to the rather large number of *relatos* of the Revolution. But it is important not simply because it is modern. Rather than a presentation of what the author has seen, multiple point-of-view moves toward an appreciation of wholeness, by exposing various facets of a circumstance, a result that resembles the political quest for national unity during the Avila Camacho administration (via the convocation of the ex-presidents). It is true that Revueltas works against his own enterprise by injecting his ideas with inordinate frequency and in a sermonizing fashion, on politics, social justice, theology, human relations, or the abuse of alcohol. However, the narrator's reference to the Revolution is an example of the broader perspective that he creates. Instead of a *relato* that tells of the Revolution "as I saw it" or "as X told me about it," Revueltas brings in the Revolution, through flashbacks, as a way of explaining certain conditions that exist during the novel's present time.

This narrative structure (the sequence in which the events are related) contributes toward our understanding of the essential nature of the circumstance in which the characters find themselves at the beginning and at the end of the novel. The key word here is "essential;" that is, an appreciation that goes beneath surface characteristics. "Essentialization" of the Mexican circumstance is the preeminent quality in novels of transcendent regionalism. It is an investigation/interpretation that makes a specific, regional circumstance comprehensible in general terms.

Revueltas works toward this goal through a kind of lyrical style, not always effective, that bears a certain resemblance to some of the poetic prose passages of Agustín Yáñez. The opening paragraph of *El luto humano*, for example, is devoted entirely to the creation of atmosphere, the feeling that prevails among the people in the room with the dying child. Objects are mentioned, but the essential quality of the situation is communicated by a combination of color, sound, odors, with an appropriate use of repetition.

Agustín Yáñez, four years later, created the atmosphere of a town in *Al filo del agua*, producing an even more complicated essentialization of place and time. In the well known "Acto preparatorio" of Yáñez's novel, both time and space are generalized by the use of several stylistic devices, the first of which is the establishment of a leitmotiv: "town of women in mourning clothes" (3). Then he creates a sense of movement in space by using adverbs of place (here, there), rather than verbs of motion. Through reference to different stages in the course of a day's passing (morning, midday, etc.), movement in time becomes a factor in the reader's experience.

An important strategy in this abstraction of reality is the absence of finite verbs. If verbs were used, one would expect a subject that, even while remaining anonymous, would have an implied individual identity. Quite to the contrary, Yáñez has communicated the essential quality of a situation that any Mexican reader would identify as Mexican, and any non-Mexican reader would accept as a credible human circumstance.

Lack of specificity in the "Acto preparatorio" recalls the elusive quality of vanguardist narrative. This introductory chapter of *Al filo del agua* was, in fact, written years before the publication of the novel, and its use during the late nineteen-forties establishes an unequivocal link between the "new novel" of this later period and the cosmopolitanism found in the vanguardist novel of two decades earlier. In fact, the course of Yáñez's career is particularly significant with regard to the changes in fiction and in politics during those years of vanguardism and internationalization.

Yáñez, along with some friends in Guadalajara, founded the magazine *Bandera de Provincias*, in 1929. Their purpose was to effect, in that city, what *Contemporáneos* was doing in the capital. The young writers associated with both reviews acknowledged their admiration for the Spanish *Revista de Occidente*. *Bandera de Provincias* was quite daring, even to the point of publishing translations of some passages of *Finnegan's Wake*. In 1930, Yáñez published a story, "Baralipton," in the magazine *Campo*. This work, which may be described succinctly as belonging to the Jarnés/Giraudoux connection, is recognized by the novelist as his entrance into literature (he had published some earlier fiction which he regarded as experiments that should be forgotten). Strangely enough, after "Baralipton," he published no fiction for ten years. When questioned about this silence, in a famous interview by Emmanuel Carballo, Yáñez explained that he had written some essays on philosophy; then he continued: "They were difficult, hard years. After the disappearance of *Contemporáneos*, there were hardly any magazines worthy of the name. During that decade, there was an attempt to organize, to direct art, a procedure that I considered, and still consider, absurd" (Carballo, 366-367). Certainly this statement refers to the official sponsorship of art that would support socialist ideology. However, this position taken by the novelist does not represent a lack of interest in Mexican reality. In the same interview, Carballo asked him how he saw the musician Gabriel in Yáñez's second novel, *La creación* (1959), and the reply was, "I see Gabriel, following the events in *Al filo del agua* and his years of apprenticeship in Europe, as a type dissatisfied with the musical techniques of a European kind and who tries, nevertheless, to use these techniques for the creation of music with a Mexican spirit. His struggle is the Mexican's struggle to find the forms of a typically national message" (Carballo, 373). There can be little doubt of a parallel between Gabriel's creation of music and Yáñez's creation of narrative. This statement indicates exactly the quality of essentialization that characterized the innovative art of the forties, and relates it to the vanguardism of a decade or so earlier. Actually, according to the novelist, he did finish writing *Flor de juegos antiguos* and *Pasión y convalescencia* during the decade of "silence" (367). These works and *Genio y figuras de Guadalajara* (1941) all qualify as essentializations, and it is important that some of them were written as early as 1927 and 1928 (367).

In addition to this link with the vanguardists, *Al filo del agua* is innovative in several other ways that contribute to the essentialization of Mexican reality. Yáñez's use of indirect free style enables his reader to experience the intimate reality of its characters. This strategy is especially important in the first chapter, following the "Acto preparatorio," where the private worlds of four very different people establish a background for the life of the town. The chapter functions as a bridge between the generality of the "Acto" and the specificity of events. However, Yáñez always sustains the feeling of essentiality by emphasizing the common human qualities that act as a basis for deeds performed. The many insights deal with religion, human love in all its manifestations, power, repression, and above all, the creative impulse. Gabriel communicates the depth of his feeling through his job as bellringer. When the Revolution comes, it functions as a means of opening up the town's hermetic society. As in *El luto humano*, the Revolution no longer produces a cathartic *relato*; it has become an organic factor in a comprehensive narrative.

Such a change in the role of the Revolution is not apparent in absolutely all novels in the nineteen-forties and nineteen-fifties, but it is manifested with enough frequency to be considered a trend. *La Negra Angustias* (1944), by Francisco Rojas González, is really a psychological study of a female revolutionary leader. Although there is plenty of action in the novel — much of it violent — when all is said and done, the book is a character study. Similarly, in *La escondida* (1948), Miguel N. Lira uses the Revolution as a context for narrating a love affair between two people of different social classes. A decade later, right at the end of the period under consideration here, Lira published *Mientras la muerte llega*, a novel in which a fictitious character looks back on his participation in the Revolution. This narrative situation is more analytical than the *relato's* projection of real, personal experience; it resembles more closely the treatment of the Revolution in Carlos Fuentes' *La muerte de Artemio Cruz* and Héctor Raúl Almanza's *Detrás del espejo*, both published in 1962.

In 1946, Mexico's dominant political party, the Partido de la Revolución Mexicana, changed its name to the Partido Revolucionario Institucional, a reflection of the trend, seen in novels, to consider the Revolution an accomplished fact. In international affairs, the nation had moved from declaration of war, in 1942, plus discontinuing diplomatic relations with Vichy France and renewing them with the U.S.S.R., to calculating the cost of the war, in 1948. Meanwhile, the need for encouragement of technical and professional preparation was recognized, Presidents Alemán and Truman had met twice, Mexico had obtained funds from the United States for purposes of industrialization, land was taken from *ejidatarios* who did not work it, and Mexico experienced a seriously negative trade balance. Obviously, the nation had moved far away from the policies of the Cárdenas era. The Revolution continued to play an important role in political rhetoric, but it was treated, in practice, as an accomplished fact, just as in the novels. Such an understanding of the Revolution does not deny its vital force, but this force was like one that stems from a cause identifiable in past history.

The change in the way novels dealt with the Revolution is one aspect of the essentialization of Mexican reality, but other factors are equally important. The narrative strategies noted especially in

El luto humano and *Al filo del agua* can be referred to accurately as "modern techniques." Innovation in prose fiction, as well as in the politics of a nation, may be effected by influence or by invention. In the analysis of either politics or novels, there is ample opportunity for discussion concerning which agent (influence or invention) has caused a specific change. In the case of Mexico, during this period, identification of the agent is less important than the fact that innovation, at this time, related Mexico to the international complex of countries, regardless of whether the change was the result of a received influence or of an invention within Mexican society.

The contrast in the political life of the nation was based on the difference between the policies of two strong presidents, Cárdenas and Alemán. A metaphor of this contrast might be structuralist-versus-monetarist, though it should be understood that the difference does not identify an administration categorically; the two sides may be represented by different agencies within a single administration (Basáñez, 67-69). Another metaphor, nationalism-versus-internationalism, is not too far-fetched, and this is the version that reveals most clearly the analogy between novel and politics during this period of gradual change toward internationalism.

In the panorama of novels published during this period, those that accomplish an essentialization of Mexican reality are accompanied by others that produce an entirely different effect: still an occasional *relato* of the Revolution, *indigenista* novels (some of which essentialize the situation rather successfully, e.g., *Los peregrinos inmóviles*, 1944, by Gregorio López y Fuentes), and novels of protest. The latter are especially significant as the opposite number to novels like *Al filo del agua*, because they are the epitome of specificity, as contrasted with the generality (abstraction) of the novels that essentialize Mexican reality. For the most part, they refer to life in Mexico City, and their dates of publication show them distributed over most of this period, with some degree of concentration in the years of the Alemán administration, for example: *Los olvidados* (1944) by Jesús R. Guerrero, *La barriada* (1948) by Benigno Corona Rojas, *El sol sale para todos* (1948) by

Felipe García Arroyo, *Río humano* (1949) by Rogelio Barriga Rivas, *Los pies descalzos* (1950) by Luis Enrique Erro, and *Candelaria de los Patos* (1952) by Héctor Raúl Almanza.

These novels tend to be exposés of the miserable, sometimes subhuman, living conditions among the poor in Mexico City. They show the author's indignation, but generally speaking, do not attempt to persuade via carefully managed narrative strategies. Rather, they are directly representational and clearly belong to the nationalist side of the contrast. On the other hand, the fact that they are about the city is significant because the trend toward internationalization turned the spotlight on the capital of Mexico, producing *Casi el paraíso* (1956), by Luis Spota and *La región más transparente* (1958), by Carlos Fuentes. These two novels, especially the latter, accomplish an essentialization of the city that corresponds to the essentialization of the town in *Al filo del agua*, an effect that is quite different from a novel of protest.

The relationship between *Al filo del agua* and the vanguardist novels of the nineteen-twenties and nineteen-thirties was underscored by the publication of a few narratives that followed the earlier mode, without emphasis on interpretation of what was recognizably Mexican. Prominent among them was Efrén Hernández's *novella, Cerrazón sobre Nicomaco* (1947), a wildly imaginative work that explains why some of Mexico's most innovative writers have considered Hernández a source of inspiration and support. The protagonist forgets to go downstairs before leaving a building that is located across from the Alameda. He lands, unharmed, in that famous park, but must recover the contents of a package which his bureaucratic superior has ordered him to deliver. All too credibly, the bureaucrat had stated, absurdly, that he was not at liberty to reveal the name and address of the person to whom the package was to be delivered. Later on, the same protagonist goes to the top of the monument to the Independence to spy on his wife whom he suspects of having an affair with a kangaroo. In a novel of standard length, *La paloma, el sótano y la torre* (1949), Hernández's imagination is somewhat more restrained, and the theme is more specifically Mexican (the coming of the revolutionaries to the town, for instance), so this work resembles more closely those narratives that essentialize Mexican reality. A more important feature of Hernández's work is its similarity to vanguardist narrative, especially with regard to "decharacterization," the diminishing (erasure) of the defining lines of character as the situation becomes more and more abstracted. Such a quality of indefiniteness may describe any of the components of narration, not just characterization, and it is fundamental to the essentializing process. The effacing of some generally accepted line becomes the key, whether it be the line of character portrayal, or of time, or of scope (for example, the "invasion" of the *norteños*, in the first part of *Al filo del agua*, melds into, becomes, the invasion of the revolutionaries, in the second part). In *Pedro Páramo*, not only is the line between past and present obliterated, so also is the line between life and death. And in *La región más transparente*, the line between the indigenous heritage and the European tradition is challenged by the presence of Ixca Cienfuegos, whose delineation as a character becomes even hazier.

An understanding of this effect in narrative may be enhanced by reference to several painting of the same period. José Clemente Orozco's "Culto a Huichilobos": serie tehules (sic, on the identification card in the Museo de Arte Moderno, Mexico City), dated 1949, portrays figures that are not specifically representational, but still are not quite abstracted. They are unquestionably human figures although they are not identified from each other, and they are part of a phenomenon that is identifiable as Mexican. This mode seems very similar to the essentializing process in *Al filo del agua* or *Pedro Páramo*; that is, the picture is not an anthropological documentary, but the essence (feeling) of a folkloric ceremony. Incidentally, Orozco used *piroxilina y temple* on masonite, a medium that is modern, as are the structures of the novels. (An earlier use of these media, possibly the first in Mexico, was by David Alfaro Siqueiros, for his "Alegoría de la igualdad y confraternidad de las razas blanca y negra en Cuba," 1943.)

The Museo de Arte Moderno also owns two oils by Ricardo Martínez that show the same kind of essentialization: "Dos figuras" (1948) and "El brujo" (not dated). The latter is an interpretation of the folkloric sorcerer in which the line of the figure all but disappears. In the top part of the painting, there is a general outline of a head — dark, foreboding, domineering. The painting then spreads out, opening into brilliant color devoid of body line. "Dos figuras" is not at all folkloric. A man and a woman, presumably lovers, are identifiable as male and female, in an overall impression of gray, as the lines of their bodies tend to vanish, in a kind of visual decharacterization, similar to the literary phenomenon in vanguardist fiction. This effect is continued by Efrén Hernández in the nineteen-forties, and becomes one of the techniques by which Mexican reality is essentialized in novels like *Al filo del agua* and *Pedro Páramo*. Possibly the clearest visual analogy to the narrative effect is "Mujer con niño" (1951), by Fernando Castro Pacheco. The figures in this painting are defined sufficiently to be recognized not only as mother and child, but also as Mexican ethnic types represented by the internationally famous muralists and several other artists of the mid-twentieth century, e.g., Zuñiga, Anguiano. However, the figures in Castro Pacheco's painting are not totally defined, and although one may recognize their "Mexican-ness," the mother-and-child motif is apparent to anyone, regardless of whether or not the viewer recognizes the ethnic factor.

The other arts showed similar tendencies to essentialize their Mexican context. In writing about the history of modern dance in Mexico, Alberto Dallal refers to the founding of the Ballet Nacional de México by Guillermina Bravo, in 1948, a major step in the development of the art in Mexico. In his following description of Mexican dance expression during this period, he says "it delves into the indigenous legends and adapts them via a new, stylized conceptualization of Mexican culture" (88). A similar phenomenon in music is especially exemplified by the work of Miguel Bernal Jiménez. Several composers had used folkloric melodies with good effect. Bernal Jiménez himself had been quite successful at adapting traditional Mexican material to modern structure and idiom; in his *Tres cartas a México* (1949), abstraction reaches a high point in his reference to three different places. It is even more difficult to identify the phenomenon in poetry than it is in music, because all lyric poetry is a kind of essentialization. Nevertheless, one thinks of Andrew Debicki's analysis of a kind of internalizing in the poetry of the late nineteen-forties, and one also recalls certain poems by Octavio Paz, as well as Efraín Huerta's extraordinary essentialization of social realities (Debicki, 23-24). In theatre, it suffices to mention that Rodolfo Usigli's *El gesticulador* and *Corona de sombra* were first performed in 1947.

Juan Rulfo's *Pedro Páramo* (1955) may well be the perfect example, in literature, of the essentialization of Mexican reality. The nationalist/internationalist implications of this novel are closely related to two volumes of short stories published a few years earlier by Rulfo and by Juan José Arreola, *El llano en llamas* (1953) and *Confabulario* (1952), respectively. These volumes became convenient examples of two trends in Mexican fiction: nationalistic and cosmopolitan. To a considerable extent, such a classification can be justified, and it is also convenient because it shows the continuation of a contrast that has existed in Mexico during a large part of the twentieth century. On the other hand, these two collections exemplify convincingly the blurring of the contrast, or, to put it another way, the reconciliation of nationalism and cosmopolitanism.

While it is true that some of Arreola's most memorable stories, in *Confabulario* and in *Varia invención* (1949), seem to have little or nothing to do with what is specifically Mexican, others coincide neatly with the notion of essentialization. Stories like "La verdad os digo" rely on some kind of ingenious development that makes one think of Borges. This particular story is a play on the biblical theme of a wealthy man's inability to pass through the eye of a needle. Both theme and sense of humor are entirely universal. On the other hand, the equally clever "El guardagujas" is not only a satire on the Mexican National Railway system, it is an interpretation, an essentialization in a humorous vein, of Mexican reality. A gentler yet more incisive portrayal is found in "Hizo el bien mientras vivió," the story of a poor devil who faces the vicissitudes of daily life in Mexico.

The story material of *El llano en llamas* is clearly Mexican, but it is simplistic to think of these stories as ordinary portrayals of typically Mexican circumstances. While "Diles que no me maten," for example, does indeed suggest very special concepts of justice, vengeance, and the life/death contrast, all of them are comprehensible, albeit strange, in broader cultural contexts where their meanings may differ to varying degrees. "Luvina" portrays a desolate circumstance that could hardly fail to impress any reader. It may well interpret a situation that exists in Mexico, but it is not a picture of Mexico, nor is the circumstance confined to Mexico. In all of his stories, Rulfo employs narrative strategies that are absolutely cosmopolitan; that is, they are strategies used by his contemporaries in all countries belonging to the occidental literary tradition. In "Diles que no me maten," the sequence of events in the narrative is carefully controlled (and contrary to chronology) to emphasize the meaning of life/death and of justice. In this story, the question of what voice is narrating — when, where, and to whom — is fundamental to understanding what the story says.

Emphasis may vary, between Arreola and Rulfo, with respect to nationalism and cosmopolitanism, but careful analysis of their work will not allow classification of them as representing two entirely different currents. The most obvious categorical difference is that Rulfo's stories are rural and Arreola's are not. But even this difference requires the further explanation that Arreola's are not really urban stories; in many of them, locale is not an important consideration. It is true, on the other hand, that, in prose fiction, urbanization tended to increase as internationalism grew. In matters of public policy, the characteristics of a developing nation were apparent: major highway construction, electrification projects, negotiations with Eximbank, a new plant for the national university, political enfranchisement of women, advances in aviation, modernization of the army, a commercial treaty with Spain. This modernizing impulse, begun during the administration of Alemán, continued under his successor, Adolfo Ruiz Cortines. The emphasis is clearly not folkloric. As the novel (and painting, as well) had forecast, via the process of essentialization, the folkloric ("popular" might be better) element in Mexican reality was losing its specific definition;

its line was being blurred. This loss of specificity promoted a blending of the folkloric into another component of the culture.

Two major events occurred in 1955, halfway through the Ruiz Cortines presidency: Emmanuel Carballo and Carlos Fuentes founded the *Revista Mexicana de Literatura*, and Juan Rulfo published *Pedro Páramo*. The magazine, in the tradition of *Contemporáneos* and *El Hijo Pródigo*, promoted Mexican literature while maintaining awareness of writing in other countries. As for Rulfo's novel, while it may be considered the optimal example of Mexican reality essentialized, in more detailed description one may observe that it is many things. Certainly it is a rural novel, the last great rural novel before the flood tide of urbanism. It is also the story of an egomaniac, of an obsession, and of an eternally simmering rancor. And it is the story of a rural *cacique* (boss), of how one man deals with a band of revolutionaries, of the death of a son, of an idealized woman, and of *almas en pena* (souls in purgatory that walk the earth). Of all these subjects, three are identifiable as most typically Mexican/folkloric, in descending order to intensity: the *almas en pena*, the revolutionaries, and the *cacique*. All the other subjects are internationally understandable. One may argue that the complex of associations constitutes a very Mexican whole, but even that factor translates into kindred, though different, cultures. Rulfo's language is unique, but hard to describe. It seems stylized, suggestive of a particular social context, yet not quite a mirrored representation. It is doubtful that this extraordinary Spanish can be translated successfully into another language, but its quality can be appreciated in Spanish by a non-Mexican. While there is much in *Pedro Páramo* that is identifiably Mexican, there is also a great deal that is readily understood by non-Mexicans who, nevertheless, think of the novel as very Mexican.

The basic question of how Rulfo essentializes Mexican reality concerns primarily the three distinctive subjects indicated above: the *almas en pena*, the revolutionaries, and the *cacique*. Since the presence of *almas en pena* obviates the customary line between life and death (with respect to functioning in the "real" world of living beings), the manipulation of traditional time becomes a primary technique. Rulfo crosses the line between present and past, abusing what is normally considered proper syntax, in such a way that the difference between "was" and "is" becomes less and less significant. This erasure of the time line is consummately important. Erasure of the body line has been noted in painting, and analogized with the erasure of character line in narrative. Rulfo's erasure of the time line creates a similar effect, and it is useful to compare these phenomena — the obliteration of body, character, and time lines — with the function of Ixca Cienfuegos in Fuentes' *La región más transparente.*

As for the revolutionaries, they appear as intruders, not quite like those in *Al filo del agua*, but as a threat to the power (proprietorship) of Pedro Páramo. They are not men with a noble cause, but a force that threatens the power of the *cacique*. This *cacique*, however, shows personal weaknesses; he is aggressive, but fundamentally insecure. His inevitable response to the presence of the revolutionaries is to buy them off, own them, come out ahead of them, whatever the means. His need to possess Susana, the idealized woman, is expressed in similar ways.

The character of Pedro Páramo, the *cacique*, is projected through a series of events that take place at widely separated points in time (if one can even speak of time with respect to this novel). These points are not ordered chronologically, but in such a way that appropriate emphasis is achieved at various moments in the development of the character. One may undertake a reordering of these events, so turning the *récit* back into *histoire*, but with limited success: first, because Rulfo's effacing of sequential time makes chronology impossible, and second, because the *récit* simply does not contain all the information necessary to make a perfectly representational account, a condition sometimes attributed to post-modernist fiction. The effect created by use of these techniques is enhanced by variations in the narrative voice and in the focussing eye. Together these strategies produce a reality that is elusive if one expects a novel of customs, but is deeply comprehended if one understands it as an essentialization of a Mexican circumstance. It is an interpretation, of course, one that corresponds to the proposition that this essence is part of being Mexican. The proposition also supposes that the abstract nature of essentialization makes the condition of being Mexican communicable interculturally. Mexican public policy followed a similar path as the nation became increasingly active in international affairs, paying a great deal of attention to certain folkloric aspects of Mexican life, through museums, restorations, and investigation, while concentrating more and more on modern, urban living, so far as the actual quality of life was concerned. Institutionalization is one of the effects forecast by essentialization; both are removed from the course of daily events. The phenomenon is notable in the change of name by the dominant political party; it is also apparent in the official organization of the arts. In 1947, the government established the Academia de la Danza (Dallal, 87) and the Instituto Nacional de Bellas Artes y Literatura (Reyes Palma, 40). These events heralded a nationalistic trend of a very peculiar kind. The government intended to internationalize its national image through these institutional means. Essentialized Mexican-ness was to be made attractive to tourists, and Mexican arts were to become the basis of small, allied industries, such as publishing and recording companies (Reyes Palma, 40). It is important to note that this kind of nationalism is quite different from the leftist commitment called for by the opponents of the *Contemporáneos* group, fifteen to twenty years earlier. The new "official" nationalism was supposed to be commercially advantageous. Obviously, it created problems. Leonora Saavedra points out that, in 1949, Carlos Chávez faced the dilemma of choice between private and official patronage for the Orquesta Sinfónica de México, and that the problem was effectively solved by the founding of the Conservatory orchestra, which, for all practical purposes, joined the older group and formed the Orquesta Sinfónica Nacional. Saavedra quotes from the decree establishing the Conservatory orchestra: "The principal patron of the arts ... is the government. It is necessary to recognize that fact and accept the necessary consequences of a practical nature" (49). One might reasonably consider such institutionalization as a perversion of the essentializing process in Mexican culture.

Certainly it is ironic that Agustín Yáñez, who called official control of art "absurd," produced such a fine example of essentialization in *Al filo del agua*. Objections to this particular expression of nationalism arise, not because what it produced was bad, but because it limited the possibilities of what might have been produced. The period dealt with here corresponds roughly to the years identified by the term "National Unity." This concept is related primarily to Mexico's participation in World War II, but it was broadened to refer to a complex formulation of progressivism, in which everything was done for the good of the nation. Carlos Monsiváis notes, with respect to this period, that "increased industrialization ... instead of suppressing nationalism and national differences, stimulated them mythologically and politically by insisting on national development" (16). It is noteworthy that this kind of nationalism is itself somewhat essentialized. One should not equate it with the usual concept of flag-waving, rifle-cleaning patriotism, but define it as a formularized we-can-do-it attitude. Even though one aspect of this effort emphasized that it was very Mexican, it was, at the same time, inevitably relating Mexico to the industrialized world. The novel accomplished a similar duality via the combination of Mexican thematic material and narrative strategies that were universally employed.

The publication of *La región más transparente*, in 1958, provided a definition of what Mexico City had become, and indicated, at the very beginning of the López Mateos presidency, the emphasis on the metropolis that was to mark the era. Two years earlier, Luis Spota had published *Casi el paraíso*, an urban novel that is an interesting precursor to Fuentes', and especially as one looks at it retrospectively, while reading *Paraíso 25*, a sequel written by Spota a quarter of a century later. One could hardly say that *Casi el paraíso* is in any way essentializing. It is more in the nature of journalistic exposé, a denunciation of national and international rascals in Mexico's capital. In common with *La región más transparente*, it portrays Mexico City as definitively cosmopolitan. There are earlier Mexican novels, especially in the nineteenth and early twentieth centuries, that deal with life in the nation's capital.

Later, in much of the post-Revolution narrative, the rural situation dominates. When the city regained primary importance, it was entirely different from the tranquil capital of a half-century earlier. In *La región más transparente*, the city is a thriving commercial and cultural center. Immigrants from Europe and South America are commonplace; intellectuals discuss the meaning of being Mexican; "beautiful people" gather at gaudy parties; the aristocracy hangs on; the proletariat lives with dreams of more *pesos*; class lines tend to be blurred, while two opposing qualities, hypocrisy versus authenticity, become identifiers that are more accurate than the usual class appellations.

The single element in Fuentes' novel that most clearly relates it to the essentializing quality of other novels is the characterization of Ixca Cienfuegos. He is a man/myth who appears, as if spontaneously, wherever and whenever his contribution matters to the author's literary mural. At times, his words and actions seem bound to the circumstance in which he appears. On other occasions, he seems removed from the ordinary course of events, somehow looking at them from a detached position. And he disappears, at the end of the novel, or perhaps better, he transforms into something greater, something more comprehensive, than an individual human entity.

As for the overall narrative strategy, Fuentes makes extensive use of simultaneity; that is, he reveals what is happening in different places at one particular time. This strategy adds an important dimension to the complex portrayal of life in Mexico City. The novel recalls the work of John Dos Passos, especially because Fuentes uses newspaper headlines as a means of establishing the context within which his characters act. And the variation in style from prose poem to stark representationalism underscores the variety in characterizations — from the man/myth, Ixca Cienfuegos, to a clearly representational Federico Robles, who functions as a central figure in the narrative.

The story — at least, the representational part of it — is about the collapse of Robles' financial empire, constructed by him after the Revolution. All the significant characters are affected, in some way, by Robles' rise from a humble position in society to high-level finance, followed by failure. His return to the land with his mistress, Hortensia, an essentially (typically) Mexican woman, produces a didactic effect that combines with the role of Ixca Cienfuegos to enhance the essentializing effect of the narrative. This thematic line relates Fuentes' novel to *Pedro Páramo, Al filo del agua*, and others that create a transcendent regionalism. But it is, of course, a novel of the city. Many of its people are sophisticated moderns — that is, they are in no way folkloric — and the author's narrative procedures show his familiarity with international fiction. The city he portrays has many identifying characteristics, but it is clearly a modern metropolis.

The reality portrayed by Fuentes corresponds appropriately to the wealth of cosmopolitan novels published the same year. Josefina Vicens' *El libro vacío* is a metafiction based on an individual of no special consequence who dreams of writing a book. Somewhere within him there is a spark that indicates possibilities greater than his achievement. In *Polvos de arroz*, Sergio Galindo tells the story of an aging spinster who becomes involved in a lonely-hearts romance. In *El norte*, Emilio Carballido also deals with an irregular romantic pairing, and reveals the functioning of two strong but different egos. It is interesting that the novels by Galindo and Carballido are set partly in Mexico City and partly in the provinces, but this fact has little or nothing to do with the effects created. They are certainly not rural novels, nor are they urban novels in the sense of dealing with the problems of city life. Along with *El libro vacío*, they are novels about people who happen to be Mexican. The settings are Mexican, but the emphasis is not. One cannot reasonably deny that these narratives are about Mexico, but what one experiences in them is not regionalistically "typical." They belong to a category different not only from regionalistic fiction, they differ also from those novels that essentialize Mexican reality.

Remarkably, readers are unlikely to notice particular narrative techniques in works by these writers, though they all employ strategies associated with recent fiction. They are not innovative in the sense of inventing new narrative devices, but they are quite comfortable in their control of multiple narrative techniques.

Sergio Fernández's *Los signos perdidos*, also published in 1958, approaches the French *nouveau roman* in its lack of action. It is excruciatingly detailed in character analysis, practically devoid of plot. It may be considered more experimental than narratives by Galindo and Carballido, but not more so than Vicens' metafiction. *Los signos perdidos*, as an experimental novel, makes an interesting contrast to *La región más transparente*, a work renowned for its experimental qualities. It amounts to a difference between contemplativeness and flamboyant exposition. This final nuance to the description of narrative in 1958 makes a peculiarly suggestive reference to the politics of the López Mateos years. The novels indicate a profound consciousness of the many aspects of Mexican reality, an awareness of Mexico's place in the Western world, and a large degree of self-confidence with respect to the literary enterprise. Public policy under López Mateos showed similar characteristics. Mexico became widely recognized as a leader of the "third world;" industry and commerce, if viewed in the proper perspective, looked rather better than third world status would indicate. The president travelled extensively to other countries, entertained foreign heads of state in Mexico. The power and light industry was taken over and reorganized. Museums of archaeology and of modern art, and much work at Teotihuacán (The Pyramids) exemplified official interest in the nation's cultural heritage (essentialized). There were some problems that disturbed people who were not bemused by the brilliant surface: trouble with the railroad workers, the imprisonment of Siqueiros for "social dissolution," and perhaps most significant of all, the adoption of the law that guaranteed free textbooks, approved by the government, of course, and providing young Mexicans a view of their country as seen by the dominant Partido Revolucionario Institucional. The reaction against this program, by some sectors of society, was almost immediate, and corresponds to the sense of uneasiness that is very obvious, thematically and technically, in novels by Revueltas, Yáñez, Rulfo, Fuentes and others, and is even present, more subtly expressed, in novels as cosmopolitan as *El libro vacío* and *Los signos perdidos*. The complex projection of society effected by modern narrative strategies, exemplified especially by multiple points of view, corresponds to the political effort to take a broad view of the nation, exemplified by the convocation of ex-presidents. On the other hand, the essentializing interpretation of Mexican reality, profoundly effective in novels as a stimulator of cultural identity, foretold similar actions on the part of the government. But the latter were of an institutional nature and their effect was to provide a degree of facile reassurance in the context of deeply felt uncertainty.

Chapter 3

Rebellion and Analysis: 1962-1979
(with a glance at the following decade)

Following the period of gradual change toward internationalism (1943-1958), the Mexican novel appeared, for the most part, to have settled into a cosmopolitan mode of analysis of the human condition, with considerably more emphasis on "human" than on "Mexican." The settings were most frequently metropolitan, but even when they were provincial, the authors' subject matter and attitudes were the same. However, in spite of cosmopolitanism's predominance, there was a cleavage, in the nineteen-sixties, between the "ins" and the "outs," that sometimes took on a nationalistic nuance. The characteristics of this controversy were quite different from those of the nineteen-thirties. In those years — the period following vanguardism — nationalism in literature meant portrayal of the military phase of the Revolution, and also of the social problems that post-revolutionary governments would, presumably, address. There was also a good deal of socialistically oriented rhetoric about art for the people. This attitude was present in the literary polemics of the time, expressed by writers as disparate as Carlos Gutiérrez Cruz and Xavier Icaza, but it is doubtful that anyone seriously expected the working class to overwhelm bookstores with its custom. More was expected of the visual arts than of literature because it was supposed that mural painting would be easily accessible to the people. This emphasis continued well into the nineteen-fifties, even though it was diminishing as the essentialization of Mexican reality became predominant.

José Luis Cuevas, the well known artist, attacked the residue of nationalistic art-for-the-people, in a sharply satirical essay, "The

Cactus Curtain." He explained how a Mexican artist could mature and have his innovative impulse suffocated by official support of the "Mexican School" of art, and by the artist's limited opportunity to see work of any other kind. Promotion of the "Mexican School" by the government had become a kind of commercial enterprise during the Alemán administration; that is, the government intended the cultivation of typically Mexican art to attract tourists and undergird commercial enterprises related to artistic production (Reyes Palma, 40). On the other hand, the internationalizing impulse, a general trend of the time, was stronger in narrative than in the visual arts, thanks to the essentializing qualities in works like those of Revueltas, Yáñez, and Rulfo. Nationalism, among these writers, was not an inhibiting factor, even though it may have been interpreted as such by some others. *El luto humano*, *Al filo del agua*, and *Pedro Páramo* are nationalistic in the sense that the narratives were developed on a basis of recognizably Mexican referents. They are not chauvinistic, and they were certainly not inhibited by allegiance to a "Mexican School;" obviously, all three novelists were quite aware of non-Mexican narrative.

The *Revista Mexicana de Literatura*, founded by Carlos Fuentes and Emmanuel Carballo, in 1955, accorded well with the practice of essentialization, during its first period. During the second period, after Juan García Ponce and Tomás Segovia assumed the editorship in 1960, its policy became more aggressively internationalist and also more pretentiously intellectual. In a discussion of the writers associated with the *Revista* during this period, John Bruce-Novoa includes Juan Vicente Melo and José de la Colina in the basic group, and later adds Salvador Elizondo (6). One could argue interminably as to whether or not the writers associated with the magazine can be called a generation, but there is no doubt that they constituted a group, just as the writers associated with *Contemporáneos* may be considered a group, as Margarita Vargas-Johnson has shown. The attitude of the group toward Mexican-ness corresponds rather well to a statement by Cuevas, in his famous essay: "What I want in my country's art are broad highways leading out to the rest of the world, rather than narrow trails connecting one adobe village with another" (120, Kemp trans.). This statement expresses part of what motivated the *Revista* group, but only part. In addition to this anti-nativistic factor, one notes the attention paid, especially by García Ponce, to certain European writers (e.g., Cesare Pavese, Robert Musil, Virginia Woolf) who were not well known in Mexico. The effect of this interest was the creation of a hyper-intellectual aesthetic that produced narratives often antithetical to society's accepted mores.

One should not underestimate the importance accorded to aesthetics by this group. It may be argued that the group's canon was less anti-nationalistic than it was pro-artistic. Bruce-Novoa deals with the emphasis these writers placed on artistic process. Interestingly enough, he relies heavily on the words of a painter, Miguel Felguérez, to explain the phenomenon (every literary group seems to have its semi-official artist). The interest in process is seen clearly in the self-referential mode that became a principal characteristic of the novel toward the end of the nineteen-sixties. Paradoxically, the works of García Ponce, the group's most prominent literary figure, are among the least self-referential of the nineteen-sixties and seventies. They are intensely intellectual. The group's canon melds three characteristics: self-reference, internationalism, and intense intellectuality/aestheticism.

The *Revista* group was contemporary with, and in some respects, similar to the writers more closely associated with the Editorial de la Universidad Veracruzana, with Sergio Galindo at the center. However, the *Revista* group apparently suffered greater anxiety regarding the promotion of their ideas, and they certainly acquired more power in the publishing circles of the capital city. They have been accused of making publication difficult for writers whose work did not conform to their criteria, e.g., René Avilés Fabila, Vicente Leñero, José Agustín (Mier and Carbonell, 68 & 111). The power group, often called the "Mafia," was not firmly identified. Its membership varied, according to the positions of "ins" and "outs" at a given moment, but the objectors frequently took aim at the *Revista* group. It is significant, of course, that these writers believed they should defend a high intellectual/aesthetic standard, even though they were motivated in part by self-interest.

One cannot regard the work of the *Revista* group as especially innovative. Rather, it continued and emphasized the internationalist trend that had been developing since the nineteen-forties. The next important innovation in narrative may be specified by reference to three novels published in the middle of the nineteen-sixties: *La tumba* (1964), by José Agustín, *Gazapo* (1965), by Gustavo Sainz, and *De perfil* (1966), again by José Agustín. These three books have become the fundamental identification of a group of novels by young writers, about their own generation, and baptized by Margo Glantz as the "onda" (77-113).

Glantz's term, though disliked by some of the members to which it refers, is significant for two closely related reasons. First, the word itself, "onda," has the meaning of "wave" and suggests a shorter period than a generation. This meaning is very appropriate for use in the last third of the twentieth century, when changes come so rapidly that "generation" serves poorly. The "onda" also synthesizes the attitude and language of this sub-generational group of people who asked "Cuál es la onda?", an expression not easily translated, that is something like "What's the deal?," in the United States. But it means more because it indicates the speaker's desire to be in on the latest, to know what fascinating (and perhaps scandalous) activity invites his participation.

The novels are innovative for a number of different reasons, all of them related, in some way, to an attack on conventionality. Undoubtedly, the quality most frequently noted and enjoyed by readers is the language itself. Its basic characteristic is its fidelity to the way young people actually talked. This accuracy provides a special kind of humor, similar to that of J. D. Salinger's *Catcher in the Rye*, or Richard Gover's *One Hundred Dollar Misunderstanding*. The "onda" novelists indulged in more language play than Salinger and Gover, and probably showed more pleasure in uttering the formerly inadmissable. Their language was read with delight by some and with clicking of tongues by others. Some pointed out, with sound reasoning, that the language was faddish and endangered the longevity of the novels. In fact, some of the language has worked its way into "standard" speech. But the major contribution made by the language of the "onda" was an aperture in the wall of conventionality. The expressive possibilities of narrative fiction were increased remarkably.

A second kind of innovation by the "onda" writers was a special identification with the city, or with a part of the city in which a given writer lived. This relationship was not at all like the astonishment of one who experiences the great metropolis for the first time, nor was it the adventure that is an aspect of "making it big." The feeling was more akin to the sense of belonging that one associates with the notion of "hometown." This phenomenon, in books that are otherwise novels of the city, took the place of provincial novels, and indicates the extent to which Mexico City was becoming the dominant factor in definition of the nation, whether in prose fiction or in public policy. Miguel Basáñez, discussing the economic crisis of the nineteen-seventies, mentions the government's failure to take into account the agricultural decline since 1966 (145-146). Novels indicated, from the middle of the nineteen-fifties, this lack of attention; the "onda" novelists underlined it.

Their sense of belonging to the city is related to an act of self-identification that produced a kind of rebellion with respect to what was socially permissible, not just in language, but in actions as well. This attitude produced greater sexual freedom, a considerable burst of creative activity, and — on the negative side — the use of drugs by some people who, if they had belonged to a more restricted "onda," might have been correspondingly more circumspect. The novels of the "onda" are disrespectful of conventionalities, but only insofar as these seemed hypocritical. They did not reject all aspects of conventional society, only those they considered useless. Here again we notice the aperture, the impulse to creative change.

In the development of the three narratives cited as a means of defining the "onda," Agustín and Sainz experimented with the organization of *récit*, and commented on the process of narrating.

Sainz especially, in *Gazapo*, used different ways of telling the story, that is, different sources of narration: tape recorder, telephone, bits of conversation, for instance. Such self-conscious narration became increasingly important and, by 1967, constituted another point of narrative innovation, related to the "onda," but with somewhat different connotations. Self-conscious narration, in the fictions specifically defined as of the "onda," signified a need to examine the creative process which, by its nature, produces change. The characteristics of the "onda" narrative, underlined by the increase in narrative self-awareness, especially notable in 1967, are an unmistakable augury of the student movement in 1968 that ended in the tragedy of Tlaltelolco.

The 1968 movement was many-faceted; even after nearly two decades, discussions of it rarely offer a simple interpretation. However, no one is likely to deny that it was an effort to create an aperture in the wall of the political and cultural establishment, an effort similar to the emphasis of "onda" narrative. In the early nineteen-sixties, Mexico projected an image of development, cosmopolitanism, and self-assurance. The image was more urban than rural, and even within this urban emphasis, Mexico City far exceeded other urban areas in importance. Novels were, for the most part, set in the capital, but this characteristic was not really an important factor in their meaning. Some novels set outside the capital, like Sergio Galindo's *La comparsa* (1964) or Elena Garro's *Los recuerdos del porvenir* (1963), are quite cosmopolitan in their interpretation of Mexican reality, and entirely in accord with the prevailing mood in the nation (or perhaps, to be strictly accurate, in the sophisticated sectors of the society). The government of Adolfo López Mateos seemed blessed with the general support of the country, and confident of its contribution to the general welfare. Certain acts and problems that seemed less indicative of a healthy nation somehow failed to win primary attention, which is not to say that they went entirely unnoticed, but that they were accepted almost subliminally. Marco Antonio Campos has pointed out that the activism of 1968 was preceded by the railroad workers' strike in 1959, followed by the teachers in 1960, and the physicians in 1965 (Campos 1983, 186). One may add the imprisonment of David Alfaro Siqueiros, and the controversy over the free textbook program.

A similar kind of subliminally appreciated unrest may be found in some pre-"onda" novels, where the phenomenon may be described most accurately as "dissatisfaction." Two very different works, Carlos Fuentes' *La muerte de Artemio Cruz* (1962) and Sergio Galindo's *La comparsa*, provide interesting examples. Fuentes' novel is a carefully focussed analysis of the Revolution; focussed, that is, on the characterization of the protagonist, Artemio Cruz, and his rise from very humble beginnings to a position of great power in the business world. The narrative strategy for which this novel is famous, a tri-faceted presentation of Cruz via three narrative positions using first, second, and third persons, amounts to more than the analysis of a single life. The three facets reveal a particular personality, of course, but they relate it clearly to the larger context of the Revolution's military phase and also of the subsequently developing Mexican economy. The acquisition of power by Cruz places him on the Alemán side of the Cárdenas/Alemán contrast, and his less-than-scrupulous actions cast an unfavorable light on the industrialization/internationalist enterprise begun by the Alemán government, and continued during the years following, with varying degrees of success. In fact, the power of Artemio Cruz illustrates the equilibrium between government and private enterprise — the basis of Mexico's stability. The novel presages the demise of this happy balance, or at the very least, makes it suspect. In addition to this rather obvious meaning of the novel, the importance of the tri-faceted narrative, as a means of portraying the Revolution and its effect on society, seems to indicate a need to use special strategies in order to communicate the wholeness of the Revolution. In other words, it seems that by the time *La muerte de Artemio Cruz* was written, the meaning of the Revolution — that is, the concept of the Revolution in the consciousness of the people — may have been disintegrating in such a way that the novelist had to find a means of reconstructing it. Or to look at it in a slightly different way, Fuentes' narrative procedure may be taken as a prediction of fragmentation in the significance of the Revolution. This prediction did indeed become a fact, even to the point of the 1968 activists' making jokes at the expense of the disintegrating concept.

La comparsa operates in an entirely different way while expressing a comparable uneasiness. Galindo's setting is a small, provincial city, Jalapa. The carefully controlled time span covers two days and the intervening night, with very specific reference to the night before, and with action extending into the evening of the second day. The third night, which never ends in the novel, circles back to the first night, in the reader's frame of reference. This plot structure works in combination with a tragedy that affects the entire city; together they constitute the novel's organizing element. Within this framework, the narrative, delivered in segments of varying lengths, moves about among several groups in the town, creating an effect of simultaneity that avoids singling out any group as the focus of the novel. This combination creates a conflict between structure and disorganization that is also expressed, metaphorically, as conventionality versus spontaneity.

The occasion is Carnaval in Jalapa, an event that is celebrated not on the traditionally appointed day, but over a weekend, to avoid conflict with the Carnaval celebration in the city of Veracruz. Such displacement of the festival presumably favors commercial interests, not an especially admirable reason for the break with tradition. However, it provides an appropriate frame for the actions of many of the characters, who allow themselves liberties, in Carnaval disguise, that they would never take while they were identifiable. To accuse these people of hypocrisy would be overly harsh. They are respectable members of society who normally obey the rules of custom. The opportunity to express themselves beyond the limits of conventional restraint amounts to an aperture that is similar to the one produced by the "onda." In the case of Jalapa's Carnaval crowd, it is significant that the aperture is temporary for some, while for others, it opens the way to a different kind of life. Unquestionably, *La comparsa* communicates a feeling of social restlessness, through characterization, action, and narrative fragmentation.

The presidency changed, in 1964, from López Mateos to Gustavo Díaz Ordaz, an old-line politician and faithful bureaucrat. Nothing in his background suggested the possibility of political change. As the heir to a long tradition of stability, he was not likely to perceive the subliminal dissatisfaction manifested in some events as well as in some novels of the period. Basáñez points out that post-Revolutionary Mexico maintained an equilibrium between two conflicting bases: a populist political system ("un sistema político de masas") and a capitalist economy (174-185). This combination required that the government be supported by the people and the people, in turn, to be controlled by the government. Basáñez believes that popular support was maintained through four means: redistribution of land, labor unions, public education, and the policy of no-reelection. At the same time, the government had been able to avoid major repressive measures. (There could well be substantial disagreement about what constitutes a "major repressive measure," but it is clear that, prior to 1968, the government had not resorted to any action as drastic as the Tlaltelolco massacre.) It is true, however, that as early as the nineteen-forties, during the move toward internationalism that is apparent in novels and in public policy, the populist/capitalist equilibrium was threatened, as the government placed increasing emphasis on the capitalist component of the anomalous pair (Basáñez 181). Or as John Johnson puts it, the "urban middle sectors" held on tenaciously during the period of radical agrarianism, and took the upper hand again in the nineteen-forties (128 ff.). The growing disequilibrium remained subliminal in political perception, just as dissatisfaction remained subliminal in the experience of fiction. It is highly significant that Basáñez, in his analysis of the Mexican economy prior to 1970, writes that one sees clearly now that the "Mexican miracle" (Basáñez places the term in quotation marks: "milagro mexicano") came to an end in 1966, not in 1970 (150). Roderic Camp, a careful analyst of the exericse of power and influence in Mexico, also points out that, in the mid-sixties, "critics inside and outside the regime began to wonder whether the authoritarian pragmatism governing the rules of the political game was any longer sufficient to cope with these problems" (14). He refers to ownership of land, education, overpopulation, nutrition, and housing. A key word in Camp's statement is "wonder." This formulation, and Basáñez's as well, indicate something less than complete awareness of the crisis in the mid-sixties. Such a condition recalls the fact that the three identifying novels of the "onda" were published in 1964, 1965, and 1966, and that they were preceded by other novels in which a feeling of dissatisfaction is present, albeit not quite overtly. The attempt to maintain the effects of the populist/capitalist equilibrium, even while its disintegration was sensed, was analogous to maintaining social conventionalities that no longer contributed significantly to the quality of life. These phenomena were present in politics and in novels, respectively, but experienced only subliminally. The novels of the "onda" brought the deficiencies to center stage, in the literary realm, and a little later, so did the movement of 1968, in the political realm.

The relationship between the "onda" novels and the 1968 movement cannot be clearly appreciated if the movement is understood solely as public demonstration and subsequent repression. The novels neither proposed nor predicted mass demonstrations. However, the spirit behind the demonstrations — often forgotten in primarily political discussions — is certainly present in the novels; the two forms of expression correspond to the same complex of feelings.

Basáñez bases his account of the 1968 movement on Sergio Zermeño's division of it into four stages (Basáñez 170-174). The first stage is what occurred during the last days of July. It began as a fight between some students in the preparatory school of the National Polytechnic Institute and students in a private preparatory school. There was nothing particularly strange about this event until the first group challenged again on the following day. Although the private school students did not answer the challenge, a company of two hundred riot police attempted to occupy the Polytechnic preparatory school buildings. Three thousand students resisted.

The fight went on for several hours and finally ended when school administrators persuaded the police to withdraw.

This event raises a number of questions. One has to do with the possible reasons for resentment, on the part of the public school students, toward those in the private school. Another asks why the riot police moved against the Polytechnic students even though no fight was going on. Were they prepared to invade the schools in any case? Was the whole affair a set-up to permit a police action against the Polytechnic schools? Did this event correspond to the growing disequilibrium in the traditional populist/capitalist balance?

On July 26, a large number of Politécnico students assembled to protest the police invasion of their institution. Another group had gathered nearby to observe the anniversary of the Cuban revolution. When a segment of the student group decided to march to the Zócalo (the seat of government, in the center of the city), riot police took action against participants in the political demonstration as well as against participants in the student affair. On this occasion, the presence of riot police in the vicinity of the preparatory school of the National University brought students of this institution into the demonstration. The objects of repression now included students in both major educational institutions and also a number of political dissidents. Arrests were made at the scene and later at the homes of student leaders and leaders of the political left. The situation worsened to the point of intervention by the army and the cessation of educational activity in both institutions. The strong-arm tactics used in the course of these events indicate clearly the defensiveness of the establishment, as growing awareness of its inadequacy increased its sensitivity to the needling exemplified in the novels of the "onda."

The second stage identified by Zermeño and Basáñez, occupying much of the month of August, was less hectic though hardly less disturbing. Mass meetings continued, and culminated in a gathering estimated at four hundred thousand, in the Zócalo on August 27. The Consejo Nacional de Huelga (National Strike Committee) had been formed earlier in the month, and a list of demands was presented to the government. They included the release of political prisoners, resignation of certain specified police officials, abolition of the riot police (*granaderos*), changes in the laws concerning "social dissolution," indemnization of the families of students killed or wounded, and an investigation of the conflict and its consequences.

Obviously, the movement had changed a great deal from a fight between two groups of preparatory school students with no overt political objective. The demonstrations had become intensely politicized, and questions of social justice became a part of the discourse. The proximity of the Olympic Games, in October, undoubtedly made the authorities even more edgy, since it was important for Mexico to project an impressively positive image. At the same time, the Olympic Games were used by the dissidents as a symbol of Mexico's pretending to be something that it really was not. They said the government should be paying attention to internal problems of social welfare, instead of sponsoring an international spectacle. At one point in the history of the movement, the strength of labor might have lent support. This coalition, never fully realized, is dealt with, restrospectively, in Gerardo de la Torre's novel, *Muertes de aurora* (1980). Enrique Krauze recalls the possibility of the movement's becoming more general, in a conversation with Octavio Paz, in 1985: "... at that luminous moment in the '68 movement, there is an arc of solidarity between generations, however ephemeral it may have been" (Krauze 1). This, just after Paz had said that, while following the course of the student rebellion in Paris, he had looked for a union of students and workers that would have proved Marx right. It did not happen.

In the third period, from late August to mid-September, Basáñez sees growing dissension within the student movement. When the rector of the university said he considered the annual presidential address to have satisfied most of the students' demands, some members of the Consejo Nacional de Huelga called for a silent demonstration in which a quarter of a million people marched to the Zócalo. The protest was non-violent; nevertheless, a few days later, the army occupied the National University.

The fourth stage, a period of increasing repression, included the defense of the university's autonomy and the evacuation of the occupying forces on September 30. However, the government's strong-arm tactics were not over, and the army delivered the final blow in the Tlaltelolco massacre on October 2. The army surrounded demonstrators gathered in the Plaza of Three Cultures; firing started, inexplicably, and hundreds of students and sympathizers were killed, wounded, or arrested and never accounted for. Memories of the dead, the injured, the missing, make a mental collage of a tragedy realized, and that knowledge evokes terrifying glimpses of an occupied university, of the Paseo de la Reforma devoid of automobiles and, in their place, tanks en route to the Zócalo, of uniformed men blasting down the door of the venerable Colegio de San Ildefonso.

This tragic memory seems hardly to coincide with the jaunty satirizing of conventionality in the novels of the "onda," but the fact that they do coincide may well offer the best explanation of what happened. The movement grew, taking on political and social significance that certainly was not apparent at the beginning. Basáñez mentions several possible causes of the conflict, none of them well defined: disagreement within the government regarding the presidential succession, a government-created scenario to justify the imprisonment of leftists prior to the Olympics, an FBI program to counteract a supposed Communist conspiracy (171). None of these possibilities reaches deeply enough into the significance of 1968. The diminishing equilibrium between populism and capitalism is an obvious basic cause, even though it may not be considered a trigger. This growing imbalance made the inadequacy of the establishment increasingly apparent and, consequently, focussed the attention, especially of the younger generation, on the outmoded conventionalities of society.

Change occurs when some segment of society (class, institution, association) senses that society's creative potential is not being stimulated. At this point, one or more segments of society will initiate a change, searching for a way to break through the wall of customarily accepted behavior. The chosen course of action may be an influence or an adaptation of what has happened elsewhere, or it may be invented by the active segment(s). In either case, the result amounts to innovation in a specific place and time. It appears that such action is likely to inspire similar actions on the part of other segments of society, though it is not clear that one action really causes another, since all such similar actions may be the result of a common instigator.

If one allows the probability of an increasing restlessness in Mexico, caused by the growing disequilibrium (disregarded by an officialdom that hoped the problem would disappear), the novels of the "onda" seem clearly to be an effort to bring about change. Their disrespect toward the customs they consider meaningless, the characters' experimentation with forbidden behavior, the authors' use of colloquial language and of popular culture, their playful use of words, their self-deprecatory humor, their self-conscious commentary on the process of narrating, their experiments with narrative voice and focalization, their skeptical view (never entirely unsympathetic) of older people, all combine to differentiate these novels from their predecessors. Some novels, like *La muerte de Artemio Cruz* and *La comparsa*, reveal strong doubts about conventionality. Even more specifically, Fernando del Paso, in *José Trigo* (1966), had written a novel about railroad workers, using an unusual structure that develops a myth-like version of the worker who has migrated to Mexico City (a kind of "essentialization" similar to the treatment of the *cacique* in *Pedro Páramo*). The "onda" novels are more innovative than most of their predecessors and, in addition, maintain a humorous tone that seems quite contrary to the tragic end of the 1968 movement. However, it should be pointed out that the early demonstrations were characterized by humor quite similar to that of the "onda," expressed in mottos, placards, wisecracks, and chants. Marco Antonio Campos, in an evocative novel, *Que la carne es hierba* (1982), recalls the exultation of the early demonstrations as well as the tragedy at the end (70 ff., especially 83). The zestful, provocative spirit of the movement in its early stages may well be the quality that has had the most enduring effect on the society.

The movement ended in the Tlaltelolco massacre, or perhaps in a more official sense, on October 6 — four days after the massacre — when the Consejo Nacional de Huelga ended its activity. It would be difficult for anyone to say exactly what happened at Tlaltelolco, or exactly where the blame should be placed. On the other hand, we do know that Gustavo Díaz Ordaz was president, and as Gabriel Zaid has said, "The presidential ineptitude that provoked the student rebellion of 1968 did not end in the restoration of order by a general. It was the president who did it" (13). This statement is part of an exposition showing that, in Mexico, the president is the one who can most readily effect a *coup d'etat*. On the other hand, even given the fact that the political campaign of the Consejo seems to have been a failure, there is not the slightest doubt that the movement of 1968 altered the mores of the nation, bringing it even more clearly into the association of developed nations. It is entirely accurate to say that Mexico, more than any other nation of the so-called "developing" world, resembled France, England, the United States — not necessarily in political doctrine, but in the complex of social attitudes promoted by the various movements of 1968.

In analyzing the narrative of the "onda," one may easily underestimate the importance of its metafiction component — that is, its self-conscious narration, its commentary on its own making. This quality may be the most important indicator of a breach in the wall of conventionality, because it is an affirmation of interest in the creative process, of a kind of thirst for attention to creativity, in a society that was (and lamentably, still is) inclined to think of creativity as icing on the cake. Metafiction, however one may react to it with respect to reading pleasure, tends to make the creative act fundamental. Such narratives thus suggest the possibility of some new concept of social organization that may lead contemporary society — not just Mexico — out of the doldrums caused by systems that simply do not work. The great danger associated with the impulse that produces metafiction is its insistence on process (creative or otherwise), to the exclusion of product. This characteristic could encourage a condition of near stasis (inconclusive busy-ness) that would stimulate creative artistic activity, but might produce a dangerous indeterminacy in public policy. Whatever the results, if any, and however widespread, the presence of metafiction in the narratives of the "onda" is magnified in the novels of 1967, the year preceding the student movement, and in 1968 itself. If one is seriously interested in sequence, it is important to realize that the novels published in 1967 and 1968 were probably written, or at least conceived, before the movement materialized; therefore, the innovative impulse of these narratives preceded the corresponding demonstrations.

Reader involvement in the creative process through a narrative's emphasis on its own coming-into-being, is certainly not an invention of the nineteen-sixties, but it was widely cultivated during that decade and the one following. In Mexico, the concentration of this kind of fiction in the late nineteen-sixties emphasizes the need for a creative experience, as well as an interest in examining the nature of the creative process. Regarding self-reference — or non-referentiality with regard to anything other than self — one should consider the works that are often called "abstract," but are more cogently referred to as "actual" (as opposed to "virtual") by Sheldon Nodelman in his study of Brice Marden, David Novros, and Mark Rothko. "Actual" indicates that the painting refers to nothing other than itself, and if one can imagine a perfectly self-referential narration, a similar effect can be anticipated. However, reader participation in metafictions is usually more similar to paintings like Carlos Mérida's "El pájaro herido" (The Wounded Bird, 1962), in which the bird appears as a representational collage on *amatl*, but in a fractured condition, so that the viewer mentally reconstructs the bird, basing this participation on his repertory of knowledge. (If the viewer had never seen a bird or a picture of a bird, he would not be able to participate.) It is instructive to contrast this phenomenon with certain paintings by Vicente Rojo, which might very well be considered "actual" until one discovers that the artist has named them "Rain in Mexico City." With this knowledge added to one's repertory, the paintings really do suggest rain, but they are still not "virtual," they do not really look like rain, nor does the viewer see rain, in his mind's eye, as the viewer sees a reconstruction of Mérida's bird.)

In a different kind of painting, Gelsen Gas's "Homenaje a Magritte" (1970), the artist portrays a woman whose face is displaced, leaving the sky visible through the space that corresponds to the shape of the face. Then the viewer discovers her face, unattached, at the bottom of the painting, and mentally places it in its customary position. Lazslo Moussong, in an essay on Gas's work, observes that ". . . he makes thoughtfully detailed and exquisitely cold paintings that are interesting not because they confront the viewer with symbolic messages or invite one to formulate extra-artistic interpretations, but rather because they make one concentrate on the direct impact of the painting itself" (102). This statement indicates quite accurately the independence of a Gas painting, its ability to confine its meaning to the experience of viewing it. Even though "Homenaje a Magritte" contains certain classical allusions, it concentrates one's attention on itself, on the artistic act of its own creation, with viewer participation in the act.

A political scientist, Henry S. Kariel, makes an interesting comparison of art and politics, based on this act of participation in the process. He complains that we see the organization of works of art as different from the organization of legislative, judicial or bureaucratic arenas.

> Were we to treat every organization of life that invites the participation of our various interests as a work of art, a new standard of judging could emerge. We would have to regard activities as rational and efficient precisely insofar as they maximize participation and multiply relationships. We would then perceive the irrationality and inefficiency of predefined margins and unambiguous centers, firm boundaries and secure structures. . . . As our nouns would ineluctably turn into verbs, as we would at last not mind surrendering our monumental hopes, we would move beyond capitalized Good and Evil (86).

One might suppose that recent emphasis on reader participation in the construction of narratives would correspond to Kariel's proposition. Many innovative novels demand a degree of participation that is radically greater than that required by a "traditional" novel. Such participation in the process of narrating can be highly rewarding. On the other hand, these novels frequently come to the end of the text with no clear resolution of the story. This indeterminate state produces a certain anxiety in many readers, and counterbalances the pleasure of participating. To put it another way, process in place of product is not always satisfactory.

Four novels published in 1967 and 1968 exemplify different uses of metafiction and different degrees of emphasis on procedure as against product: *Cambio de piel* (1967) by Carlos Fuentes, *Morirás lejos* (1967) by José Emilio Pacheco, *El garabato* (1967) by Vicente Leñero, and *El hipogeo secreto* (1968) by Salvador Elizondo. These novels correspond to four different points on a scale that extends from major emphasis on resolution (with slight emphasis on procedure) to major emphasis on procedure (with slight emphasis on resolution). At the first end of the scale, the novel tells a story different from the story of its own coming-into-being, though it may allude to the latter. Danny J. Anderson explains this phenomenon in detail, using three of the novels mentioned here (he does not include *El garabato*).

Cambio de piel is especially significant because it places the reader in a position of doubting, with respect to what is fiction and what is reality. Fuentes invents a narrator who participates in some of the action and, presumably, invents the rest of the story as he tells it to another character in the novel. The consequent sense of middle ground between fiction and fact accords well with the story that combines history and myth, as Fuentes brings pre-Hispanic Mexico into the present (shades of his "Chac Mool") and also places modern Mexico in the larger context of twentieth-century Europe and United States. The novel looks into the past of four characters caught at one specific point in time and space. The story is quite attuned to its present time, as it involves some "hippie" types. The pre-Hispanic aspect contributes to a notion of sacrifice (expiation?) in connection with the overriding theme of human brutality. Obviously, this novel belongs to its time in more than one way, but for present purposes, it is important to emphasize Fuentes' ingenious use of the narrative situation to create a particular kind of experience during the act of reading. There is, of course, a great deal of "story" in *Cambio de piel*, but the process of reading is more interesting than the sheer revelations of the denouement; a reader is most likely to become involved in the puzzle of who is talking to whom, and with what authority.

Morirás lejos resembles *Cambio de piel* in some respects: it deals with an internationally significant topic (tragic episodes in the history of the Jews) and subverts the reader's normal understanding of the difference between reality and invention. However, Pacheco's novel places considerable emphasis on process, especially because it allows the reader alternatives. This indeterminacy is very postmodern in its suggestion of infinite possibilities; the great *im*possibility is specific, universal definition of outcome. The meaning depends on each reader's individual repertory. The basic situation portrays one man, secluded, looking at another who is seated in a park. One may be a Jew, the other a Nazi. But even this possible identity is brought into question as the difference between pursued and pursuer becomes clouded. Readers are confronted by a challenge to the imagination, and the challenge becomes an affirmation of the creative impulse. Resolution and/or definition are notably absent.

In *El garabato*, Leñero accomplishes the confrontation of reality/fiction by employing a Chinese box of *récits*. To explain how the procedure works, let us say that a novelist (Leñero, if you wish) receives the manuscript of a novel from Pablo Mejía H., a writer born of the author's (Leñero's) imagination. The protagonist of Mejía H.'s novel is a frustrated writer named Fernando J. Moreno, a product of Mejía H.'s imagination (and, of course, a sort of second-generation invention of the prime author [Leñero]). Within Mejía H.'s novel, a young writer named Fabián Mendizábal asks Moreno to read the manuscript of a novel written by Mendizábal. The story, then, is about the reading of two novels within a basic frame. One of the two novels is a detective story, the other is a study of personal relationships. The end of this procedure is, in some sense, an outcome. But it certainly would not satisfy traditional expectations, because, although one plot line is resolved, the other is not. One must face the problem of whether or not one conclusion prohibits the second. This quandary naturally emphasizes the nature of invention. One may say that *El garabato* is about the invention of invention, not the invention of reality. Leñero's artifice is one step removed from the invention of reality. It is the invention of invention that, in its turn, may or may not invent reality. This quality brings into focus one of the characteristics of all procedure-oriented enterprises -- that is, the possibility of being one step removed from reality, or to assume, on the other hand, that invention *is* reality (process *is* product).

The exact identification of process as product is effected about as completely in *El hipogeo secreto* as one can expect in any narrative. Since words are employed in narrative, and words function in fields of connotation, it is practically impossible to make a narrative that refers only to itself, one that is as "actual," for example, as a Rothko painting. In the case of *El hipogeo secreto*, the author has pointed out that characterization and character action are possible without portrayal of the character as "real" (Glantz, 28). This statement, of course, recognizes the supremacy of the concept of self-reference in a narrative. Steven M. Bell, in a detailed analysis of Elizondo's novel, explains the relationship between two narrative planes: one that involves characterization and another that develops self-referentiality (Bell, 48). In the final analysis, what one experiences is the act of narrating, the coming-into-being of the narrative.

Considering together these several examples of metafiction, one finds that *El hipogeo secreto* is the clearest and most extreme example of the common denominator among these novels. It is also apparent that resolution (denouement) diminishes in importance as self-referentiality increases. One may suspect that, if this kind of fiction reflects or predicts a social circumstance, the analogous representation, in society, of the literary phenomenon will be a diminution of determinacy accompanied by an increase of egocentricity/individuality. Of course, one might assume the development of yet unspecified relationships that would be indeterminate by nature and would, therefore, negate egocentricity/individuality.

In public administration, this circumstance produces indecisiveness as a result of emphasis on process at the expense of product. At the same time, persistent indeterminacy invites exercise of power by individuals who emphasize the other side of the proposition, as in the misbehavior of the executive branch of the United States government in the Iran-Contra affair.

In Mexico, the most readily apparent political change analogous to narrative emphasis on procedure was the change from traditional politician to technocrat, while the equally traditional equilibrium disappeared, as populist politics lost out to capitalist economics. This change did not take place abruptly after the events of 1968; rather, it is more to the point to consider the emphasis on metafiction in 1967 and 1968 as a forecast of the change in public policy. Of course, one's understanding of the situation must include also the novels of the "onda," since their particular combination of self-reference and joyful dissidence suggested not only the demonstrations of 1968, but the subsequent political change as well.

During the period of demonstrations in 1968, Luis Echeverría Alvarez, the Secretary of *Gobernación* (more or less corresponding to "Interior") served as the communications link between the student leaders and the government, and in the process of doing so, enhanced the possibility of his becoming a presidential candidate. The actual administration of Echeverría, beginning in 1970, suggests that he may have been a conciliatory intermediary in 1968, but the probability is that no one could have softened the hard line of Díaz Ordaz that prevailed during the rest of the latter's administration. This hard line was based on the incumbent's fear of losing some part of the legacy with which he had been entrusted, and especially to a bunch of young whippersnappers who did not show proper respect for their elders. He was probably concerned also about the apparent loss of that equilibrium between the private and public sectors that had been, for many years, the basis of Mexico's stability.

The extent to which the movement of 1968 spread beyond the university community is not clear. Certainly there were attempts to incorporate labor and agricultural leadership into the movement. In fact, one wonders if the meeting in Tlaltelolco was held in that place as a means of broadening the significance of what had already taken place. It is said that the rector of the university advised the student leaders, a few days before the Tlaltelolco massacre, to hold the meeting within the confines of the university. Even though the university's autonomy had been disregarded earlier, in an unwarranted exercise of power, a meeting held within the university would have enjoyed at least the theoretical protection of law. With regard to the participation of labor, one supposes that, whatever the efforts to enlist the cooperation of workers, their organized strength supported the government during the period of unrest (Basáñez 186).

The remainder of Díaz Ordaz's presidency was a period of strong-armed conservatism. Interestingly enough, his handpicked successor, Luis Echeverría, conducted an electoral campaign characterized by rhetoric not only conciliatory with respect to the dissident movement, but quite disturbing to the so-called private sector, that is, the industrial/commercial interests. Once in the presidency, Echeverría found it necessary to improve his relationship with this group, and employed Enrique Garza Sada, the Monterrey industrialist, as a kind of ambassador. Enrique Bonfil functioned in a similar capacity with respect to the agrarian leaders.

These declarations, attitudes, and nominations are a perfect example of emphasis on procedure rather than product, and are analogous to the procedure-oriented narratives that anticipated them. (It is important to note that this analogy is based on narrative technique, not on themes.) It would be inaccurate to claim that nothing happened during the Echeverría administration. There was, in fact, a great deal of activity among the agrarians, in the form of occupying and claiming land. But the promise of change, contained in the president's rhetoric, amounted to little or nothing. In June of 1971, a tragic clash occurred between students and "halcones" (police agents poorly disguised as civilians). Echevería promised to investigate fully this reopening of the wound of Tlaltelolco, but no such investigation was ever made public, and the whole matter disappeared from the news media. The president was forced also to rebuild the confidence of the private sector in order to prevent a flight of capital. In the middle of his term, both Garza Sada and Bonfil were assassinated.

The movement of 1968 was not effective in producing political change, but it created three important effects: (1) the public/private equilibrium would not operate as efficiently and unobtrusively as before, (2) the possibility of dissidence was established, and (3) the PRI's determination to stay in power became obvious. In other words, the public changed even if politics did not. Octavio Paz has said that 1968 initiated a period of analysis of Mexico's political system (1985, 9). That has certainly been the case, but one would never know it to be so on the basis of observable change. The process of analysis has been exactly that: process. The first indication of possible change was the relative weakness of the PRI in the 1988 presidential election.

So far as the narrative/politics analogy is concerned, the six or seven years following Echeverría were especially revealing because emphasis on process became even more apparent, and it is entirely reasonable to regard the emphasis on narrative process as a prediction of what happened in politics. Echeverría's successor, José López Portillo, was not a politician in the traditional sense. He was trained as an economist, a specialist more accustomed to planning how something should be done than in actually achieving results. The renewed interest in free enterprise also encouraged process and discussion of process, with product existing only in theory. López Portillo was followed by Miguel de la Madrid, another specialist. An important difference between the administration of Echeverría and that of López Portillo was the shift from agrarian support to labor support. Operating in conjunction with procedure-oriented bureaucrats, an aging labor leader, Fidel Velásquez, became the major figure in Mexican politics (though not the major public administrator).

López Portillo initiated a program of electoral reform that gave minority parties a small voice and a moderate amount of publicity. It also provided specialists in administration an opportunity to discuss the significance of the reform. This process has been interesting, but the product is not definable. Toward the end of his presidency, after years of indeterminacy, López Portillo took a bold step in nationalizing the banks, effecting, thereby, a product without procedure. This kind of decisive action illustrates the danger created by indeterminacy, with the caveat that the example noted here is far milder than many scenarios one might imagine. It raises grave questions about the viability of a new order based on process/participation.

The inevitably specific focus of this essay on the events of 1968 differentiates it from similar considerations of other narrative innovations that refer to more general periods of history. The specificity of 1968 has produced many novels that refer to the events of that year, as part of the process of integrating that phenomenon into the nation's awareness of itself. By the middle of the nineteen-eighties, numerous essays, lectures, and symposia had dealt with the novel and 1968. Narratives have used many different strategies in dealing with the subject, and one is tempted to say that theme is their only common denominator. However, one notes also a general interest in experimental narration which, if not really new, is certainly modern, and often becomes self-referential, to varying degrees. It seems important that not many writers dealing with Tlaltelolco have felt the need to be "realistic," in the traditional sense of the term. One of the closest to such a classification is Gonzalo Martré in his *Los símbolos transparentes* (1978), which was written several years before it was published. It is very close to the actual events, intensely erotic, and strongly denunciatory in tone. A very different novel, María Luisa Mendoza's *Con él, conmigo, con nosotros tres* (1971), is even more realistic, but in an entirely different sense. The author shares with her reader the nightmarish quality of the night of the massacre. In many other novels, the experience of the situation is delivered clearly to readers, but not in terms of objective realism.

In an excellent essay on Arturo Azuela's *Manifestación de silencios* (1979), Federico Patán explains that this novel represents a stage of contemplation of the events of 1968, in addition to describing and criticizing them. Azuela provides the description by having one of the characters read an account written by another character, a journalist. This meta-narrative effect is important since it coincides with other phenomena related to 1968. While the narrative within the narrative provides the basic information about what happened at Tlaltelolco, so establishing that event as one of the time planes used in the narration, a variety of other voices supply information that amounts to an analysis and contemplation of the events. Patán emphasizes three characters to explain how these effects are created. One is Gabriel, the journalist who, paired with Isabel, promises an activist continuation of what was started and left unfinished in 1968. Another is Domingo Buenaventura, the "historical consciousness/awareness (*conciencia*)" of the novel (Patán takes this from an interview with Azuela, published by Margarita García Flores, 97). In this characterization we encounter the important suggestion of José Revueltas and, according to the novelist, several other remarkable real-life people.

The third key personage in Patán's explication is José Augusto Banderas, who suffers personally the repression and violence of the period. These three, with a cast of supporting though certainly not minor characters, produce a convincing and deeply affecting view of the period. The only missing factor is the movement's initial joy, the surest sign of creative impulse, the will to break through — the will that supports, at the deepest level, a continuation of the movement, in spirit if not in activism.

Manifestación de silencios is not an easy novel to read. Its emotional impact is considerable and, in addition, Azuela has made an intricate pattern of changes in narrative voices and temporal planes. Although typographical indications assist the reader in appreciating this pattern, one must remain alert in order to experience the effect of the narrative collage. Patán's opinion is that "a novel with a structure made of an accumulation of fragments whose sum creates the definitive image, corresponds to a world in disintegration." He considers, therefore, that the novel's form is part of its message. One can hardly object to this formulation, but still may point out that the sum of the fragments in Azuela's novel may produce an image more definitive than any available to an observer of the world in disintegration. Actually, the fragmentation in *Manifestación de silencios* seems retrospective, more reflective than predictive. It certainly resembles, in technique, some narratives that preceded 1968 and now appear to have presaged what was to come. Its factor of self-consciousness resembles also the peculiarity of process that presages a political establishment of the same persuasion.

While the novel genre, during this period, seemed to anticipate the violence of 1968 and the subsequent bureaucratic stasis (the emphasis on procedure and the rise to power of the technocrats) there was nothing in the novel to suggest the strong-arm brutality with which the movement was repressed, unless one should assume that a conservative establishment will always respond violently to teasing by a disrespectful subordinate. In connection with the idea of repression, some novels were written — even while Tlaltelolco was being analyzed, criticized, and reconsidered — that seemed to forecast a very conservative, perhaps repressive, governmental position. This innovation in narrative is in a process of identifying itself as the present essay is being written, and its relationship to politics is still in a speculative stage, but some general comment may be significant.

Two aspects of recent fiction appear to suggest conservative politics: one is thematic; the other, technical. The thematic factor is made up of history and nostalgia. Historical novels like Eugenio's Aguirre's *Gonzalo Guerrero* (1980), Silvia Molina's *Ascensión Tun* (1981), and Fernando del Paso's *Noticias del imperio* (1987), dealing with widely separated periods in Mexico's past, all belong to a national identity search, and indicate a desire to hold on to one's heritage. This phenomenon alone would not necessarily suggest conservative politics, but it is reinforced by novels that offer nostalgic views of the authors' generational experiences. Campos' *Que la carne es hierba* is an example, along with many others including María Luisa Puga's *Pánico o peligro* (1983) and Héctor Manjarrez's *Pasaban en silencio nuestros dioses* (1987). Both narrative examinations and reconstructions, of the distant past and of the recent past, seem to be ways of searching for something that can be identified as reliable. One notes also a presence of the parapsychological (some might prefer "mystical" or "magical") that may represent another way of searching for something more stable than the inconstant reality of daily life; for example, Joaquín-Armando Chacón's *Las amarras terrestres* (1982), Francisco Prieto's *Si llegamos a diciembre* (1985), and Ignacio Solares' *Casas de encantamiento* (1987), the last a combination of parapsychology and nostalgia.

As for narrative technique, recently many novelists have "gone back to telling stories," as some of them put it. By this statement, they mean that they have given up narrative gamesmanship and chosen to recount the actions of recognizable characters in credible situations. This trend obviously recalls the kind of novel that is generally described as "traditional," and one might assume, erroneously, that such novelists were reverting to an old-fashioned narrative mode. Actually, many different narrative strategies have been introduced or have been especially emphasized since the heyday of nineteenth-century realism, and these cherished narrative tools could not be put aside easily. The case is simply that these novels seem "traditional" enough — largely because they are more easily accessible — to suggest a conservative bent.

Obviously, this apparently conservative trend is antithetical to the cultivation of fiction for its own sake or of fiction that forces readers to act as organizing agents. On the back cover of Solares' first novel, *Puerta del cielo* (1976), Salvador Elizondo, the author of one of the most perfect self-referential narratives, praises Solares' novel as a "well considered corrective to the excesses of a highly intellectualized but opaque narrative." Self-conscious narrative has persisted, of course, just as all tendencies in fiction continue beyond the starting point of another trend. The issue is complicated, however, by another factor: the adventurous fragmentation of narrative to the extent that reconstruction of an *histoire* is not only im-

possible, it is not even a matter for consideration. One may use-
fully compare Gustavo Sainz's *Fantasmas aztecas* (1979) with Car-
men Boullosa's *Mejor desaparece* (1987). Sainz's novel suggests a
story that is never really told; readers will likely be aware that
somewhere, behind or beyond what is being read, there is a story.
By contrast, *Mejor desaparece* is a series of vaguely connected
episodes that communicate feelings, but offer no possibility of logical sequence.

Federico Patán suggests, in his analysis of *Manifestación de silencios*, that fragmented narrative corresponds to a fragmented society. If that is the case, works like *Mejor desaparece* must presage
even greater social fragmentation. This possibility is entirely in accord with some notions of post-modernism. The openness of such
narratives, and of such a society, invites the hope for a new politics
— even more, a new configuration of relationships — as set forth by
Henry S. Kariel. However, it would be inappropriate to suppose
that Mexican narrative promises any such development, since it is
obvious that the openness on one side is counterbalanced — more
likely, overbalanced — by closure on the other. To put it another
way, the acceptance of process is counterbalanced — or overbalanced — by the desire for product.

The 1988 presidential election was an interesting political manifestation of this ambivalence. Carlos Salinas de Gortari, a specialist like his two immediate predecessors, was elected by the smallest
officially announced margin in post-revolutionary Mexico. The
major challenge to him was the candidacy of Cuautémoc Cárdenas,
an active member of the PRI until the frustration of his reform
movement within the party made his separation from it necessary.
With regard to the movement, one of Peter H. Smith's conclusions
is highly significant:

> . . . I do not believe that the struggle [the contest for power] takes place be-
> tween the three components of the PRI — the peasant, worker, and popular
> sectors — or that Mexico has developed (or is developing) a one-party
> democracy. Rather, the political process entails an unceasing battle between
> factional *camarillas*, groups bound by loyalty to an individual leader . . . who
> is expected to award patronage in return for their support. . . . In important

(and revealing) ways, these attachments bear close resemblance to the *caudillismo* of years past (50-51).

So there was, in the 1988 Cárdenas campaign, a mixture of tradition and innovation. He headed a faction within the party that was made cohesive by a combination of his charisma and his ideology. His work within the party had a traditional quality that is analogous to those narratives that, for nearly a decade, have used some new techniques while holding on to the past, thematically, and creating an impression of being a "traditional" novel. But Cárdenas and his followers were forced to break with the party, to fragment it, so to speak, in a way that corresponds to the non-traditional side of narratives since the nineteen-sixties. One notes again the contrast between openness and closure.

Paradoxically — or apparently so — the Cárdenas challenge, which one must see as openness, ran counter to the emphasis on process, which one must also consider openness, that characterizes the administrations of specialists (*tecnócratas*). True paradox was obviated by the fact that the process which characterized the administrations by specialists was a process of rhetoric rather than of genuine openness that is associated with participation. The risk of openness/indeterminacy has been noted in the precipitate action of López-Portillo. One must beware of impulsively realized product-without-process in the present fragmented situation.

It would be foolhardy to write about the novel and the future of Mexico without mentioning Carlos Fuentes' *Cristóbal Nonato* (1987). This novel is not related to the principle of innovation and analogy that constitutes the basis of the present study. However, it may be taken as a prophecy or warning that projects the dark side of Mexico's future, what might be called "the worst scenario." Fuentes exploits his tremendous imagination in a display of verbal games that become excessive for some readers. For many Mexicans, these games cast a jocular shading upon a very serious accusation. The fact that Fuentes has spent much of his life outside of Mexico makes this combination especially irritating to those who feel deeply the new version of nationalism. On the other hand,

Fuentes is not alone in his grave disapproval of the state of affairs in the republic and especially in its capital city. Novelists who are intimately associated with Mexican reality have deplored the present situation even if they have not forecast greater tragedy — for example, two very different novels, Carlos Eduardo Turón's *Sobre esta piedra* (1981) and José Agustín's *Cerca del fuego* (1986). The first is an inelegant but disturbing narrative that discovers corruption in almost every sector of society; José Agustín's is a clever combination of satire and black humor that portrays the horrors of a metropolis in decay and the vulnerability of self-referential narrative (another way of decrying process).

Denunciatory novels are significant, of course, but they are not necessarily related to innovation. Their themes do constitute something of a new factor in Mexican fiction, or perhaps it might be better to consider them another kind of reversion to the past. In any case, those qualities in the novel that indicate the conservative desire to stay within a tradition, albeit with moderate change, appear stronger than the inclination to change radically. This conservatism coincides also with a recently apparent nuance of ever changing nationalism — one that seems related to the nation's economic problems. This neo-nationalism is observable in an increased awareness of Mexican tradition, probably sponsored by the risk of losing national identity because of the economic crisis. On the other hand, fragmentation and the possibility of radical process/indeterminacy persist, although in what seems to be a secondary position. The present indications offered by a reading of narrative suggest the greater likelihood of a conservative, possibly even a repressive, political situation. However, since the indications are not entirely clear, analysis rather than divination of the novel's role in society since 1979 must await the passage of time.

Chapter Four

A Century of Plans: 1816-1895

Any one of three instances of narrative innovation in the twentieth century could be said to mark the beginning of modern Mexico. All of them postdate the Revolution. They have occurred at intervals of approximately twenty years, and all three have been concerned, in one way or another, with the role of internationalism. The earliest of these periods, generally called "vanguardist," was dominated by writers who intended to make Mexican literature as modern — and as cosmopolitan — as European letters. Such an undertaking may seem strange in view of the inevitably nationalistic quality of the Revolution. However, one aspect of the revolutionary enterprise was to awaken Mexico from the passivity of Porfirio Díaz's outwardly benevolent dictatorship. The intellectual/artistic project of modernization began during the waning years of the Díaz regime and initiated a period of literary experimentation in the nineteen-twenties and thirties. The vanguardists, of course, were criticized bitterly by many who were nationalistically inclined.

The second period of innovation, in the nineteen-forties and fifties, was fundamentally a reaffirmation of the earlier vanguardism, but with an important addition: the successful combination of Mexican subject matter with modern narrative techniques. By the late nineteen-sixties, the center point of the third period of narrative innovation, internationalism was such a generally accepted phenomenon that its ratio to nationalism was not a basic issue. This circumstance alone may be taken as an indication of modernity, or national maturity. Such an appreciation must certainly be enhanced by the self-analysis of this period. Of course, there was, and still is, discussion of the nationalist/cosmopolitan divergence. José Luis Cuevas wrote a famous essay, "The Cactus

Curtain," in which he complained of official emphasis on nationalist themes. Juan Bruce-Novoa sees him as something of a forerunner to the literary coterie headed by Juan García Ponce (the group associated with the second period of the *Revista Mexicana de Literatura*). The concern of these writers, however, was not purely a question of nationalism versus cosmopolitanism; rather, it was a matter of the nature and significance of art.

The narrative innovations during these three periods make interesting analogies with changes in public policy, and frequently the literary manifestation precedes its political counterpart. This sequence may be characteristic of twentieth-century Mexican society, so distinguishing it from Mexican society of earlier periods. While there are clear associations, in the nineteenth century, between the realms of narrative and of politics, it is generally easier to see nineteenth-century narrative innovations as reflecting political change rather than presaging it.

Unlike the twentieth century, in which large numbers of novels enable one to discern trends with reasonable accuracy, nineteenth-century Mexico offers relatively few novels before mid-century. It is also true that Mexico projected a very unstable national identity before mid-century. It was a period of continual conflict between federalism and centralism, with public policy determined more often by the power of a prevailing leader than by coherent policy. This state of confusion, of undefined or uncertain policy, produced dissatisfaction among the *yanquis* who had settled in Texas, caused them to declare independence, and eventually led to the war between Mexico and the United States. The novels of José Joaquín Fernández de Lizardi, especially *El Periquillo Sarniento* (1816), may be seen as anticipating, at least to some degree, the chaotic conditions of those early years. A few other novels may well reflect the conditions of the time, but they are so few in number that generalization is not practical. Trends can be identified in the burst of literary activity following the restoration of the republic (in the late eighteen-sixties, after the Reform and the French Intervention). From that time on, the narrative genre is a good deal richer, but even so, sporadic clustering is likely to create distortions in one's view of relationships between narrative and the other constituents of society. Of course, this very condition of clustering in the writing of the narrative probably corresponds to Mexico's irregular progress toward national maturity. During the earlier half of the century, in addition to *El Periquillo Sarniento*, Manuel Payno's *El fistol del diablo* (1845-1846) must be considered because of its obvious relationship to the political/social context, whether or not it can be considered as anticipating political change. Later on, in the middle of Maximilian's short-lived empire, Luis G. Inclán published *Astucia* (1865), a novel related to *El Periquillo Sarniento* and to *El fistol del diablo* by its criticism of society's folly, but obviously at odds with the organization of the country by the leaders of the Reform.

José Joaquín Fernández de Lizardi ("El Pensador Mexicano") set his *El Periquillo Sarniento* in the early years of the nineteenth century, using the traditional picaresque mode as a vehicle for exposing certain social deficiencies of the time. Standard criticism and analysis of *El Periquillo Sarniento* identify it as an imitation of a Spanish picaresque novel, with didactic passages concerning Mexican society and, in a more general way, the human condition. Feijoo and Rousseau are recognized (emphasized especially by J. R. Spell) as major influences on the author's ideas. The accepted view has been that Fernández de Lizardi's instructive disquisitions — delivered, in the *récit*, by the reformed picaro, Periquillo, to his children — detract from the novel's interest as narrative. These studies have also pointed out linguistic Mexicanisms as well as the social problems dealt with.

More recently, Nancy Vogeley has reopened the case of *El Periquillo Sarniento*, proposing that traditional criticism of the novel has evaluated it, to its disadvantage, against a standard that is European rather than American. In her essay on Fernández de Lizardi's concept of "the people," she contrasts the difference between the relative linguistic/social homogeneity of Spain with the Mexican situation where "there was no peasantry; instead, labor was done by Indians who spoke Indian languages or pidgin Spanish, and blacks whose oral tradition in Spanish was limited" (460). It follows logically that these people would have a poorly developed sense of patriotism, even if such a sense existed at all. The people, as shown by Fernández de Lizardi, would certainly be led easily by strong individuals, and that is exactly what happened after independence was achieved. Egocentric, personalistic leadership dominated the scene.

It is important to note the relationship between Fernández de Lizardi's work and the stages of the Independence movement, especially because the working class took a primary role in the Hidalgo rebellion. The first edition of *El Periquillo Sarniento* appeared in 1816, minus the fourth volume which was suppressed by the censors. The novelist may well have thought earlier of turning to narrative fiction as censorship limited his journalistic activities (Spell, 31-32). In any case, the setting of his novel is around 1810, the time of the Hidalgo revolt. Vogeley also notes important references to "the people," in journalistic writings by Fernández de Lizardi, prior to publication of the novel. Though with absolutely no intention of claiming that the novelist referred directly to the followers of Father Hidalgo, one notes that this first movement toward independence was the only people's rebellion in the Spanish-American struggle for freedom from Spain. Even in this case, the motivation is clouded by the fact that Father Hidalgo acted on the basis of readings that certainly were not addressed to the requirements of an American "people."

The Hidalgo rebellion was more concerned with reform than with independence. The priest of Dolores (Hidalgo) joined a group of *criollos* (people of Spanish ancestry, born in Mexico), in Querétaro, who favored equality between the colony and the mother country. One specific requirement was that the colonial government not be in the hands of bureaucrats sent from Spain. Father Hidalgo had a special interest in this provision because some of his work had been negated by such authorities. Never one to respect unreasonable legalities, he had taught the native Mexicans of his parish to be horticulturists and artisans. The viceregal government, preferring that the native peoples not be given such an opportunity to improve their condition, ordered the destruction of these projects. Hidalgo and his friends in Querétaro planned a rebellion to take place in December of 1810. Their plan was to seek the collaboration of the *criollos* in the region. However, their intent was made known to the authorities toward the middle of September, and Hidalgo responded in great haste by calling his parishioners together. As Henry Bamford Parkes puts it, "But the whole plan had to be changed. It was impossible now to organize a creole rebellion or to hope to seduce the army. Without weapons or allies, they could only appeal to the Indians and to the resentment engendered by centuries of oppression" (146). So this people's army was assembled, made up of resentful workers united not by the dream of making a new nation, but by rhetoric assuring them that their religion (the religion that had given them a better livelihood) had been betrayed by the Spanish authorities. Their banner was not political; it was a likeness of the Virgin of Guadalupe.

In telling his own story, Periquillo does not address the nature of the Hidalgo rebellion. He does say a good deal about the less fortunate classes in the city, and one of his complaints is their ignorance. As Vogeley observes in her study, *Fernández de Lizardi*, via his protagonist-narrator, shows some ambivalence in his evaluation of the lower classes. Depravity, poverty, and ignorance seem alternately to join and separate as he searches for terms that will define his concerns. However one understands Fernández de Lizardi's work, there can be no doubt that he was deeply concerned about the ignorance of the people. It is also obvious that the people making up the Hidalgo army did not have the information necessary to make them "patriots" of that period of liberation. This condition became a fundamental problem of national Mexico; the people, in the large sense, were simply not included. To make matters worse, the ideological lines identifying Spaniards and *criollos* were not clearly drawn. *El Periquillo Sarniento* displays well the opportunism and corruption that became pervasive factors in Mexican life and literature.

Fernández de Lizardi's fiction, read in conjunction with some of his more journalistic writing, projects his advocacy of a quality that can best be identified as "common sense," and this attitude extended to his statements about religion. Father Hidalgo would naturally enjoy the novelist's approval, given the cleric's practical approach to the welfare of his parishioners. One thinks of later fictional characterizations of this quality, in Nicolás Pizarro's *El monedero* (1861) and Ignacio M. Altamirano's *La Navidad en las montañas* (1870). In both novels, a priest is duly concerned for the earthly welfare of his flock; in Pizarro's novel, Padre Luis establishes a cooperative society that suggests Father Hidalgo's efforts in Dolores. Vogeley points out that, in his notes to *El Periquillo Sarniento*, Fernández de Lizardi (the writer himself, not his narrator-protagonist) joins his invented characters in projecting how the lower classes might be incorporated into a new kind of society:

> Under the new system in which agriculture would replace mining as the principal source of wealth and unproductive members of society such as the nobility would work, the lower classes would be educated to be sober, honest and hard-working. Lizardi is optimistic that the manual skill which they presently display, the instinctual kindness and sense of rectitude that he often attributes to them, are evidence of their educability (Vogeley, 463).

Vogeley also notes that "the picaresque adventures of Periquillo are representative of the situation of many *criollo* youths whose family background and education did not equip them for the corruption and ignorance they encountered" (461). It might be added that these victims, if they were like Periquillo, became effective collaborators. The story does not communicate glittering promise for a new nation. Indeed, the conflicting form and content that cause so much trouble in dealing with this book represent a combination of conservatism and progressivism that was present in the campaign for independence and was at the heart of the new nation's problems. Even while criticizing an existing order and suggesting the possibility of a new one, the author chose, as his medium, a mode inextricably related to traditional Hispanic culture.

The struggle for independence dragged on, with another priest, José María Morelos, assuming leadership after the defeat of Hidalgo. The effort was always inhibited by uncertainty and disagreement about the nature of Mexico's relationship with the past: whether the goal was independence or equality, whether allegiance was owed to Fernando VII or to the *Cortes* (parliament), whether Mexico was to be a kingdom or a republic. When independence was finally achieved, it was by means of a coalition of conservatism and progressivism — a worthy reflection of the two aspects of *El Periquillo Sarniento* — after Agustín de Iturbide and Vicente Guerrero made their peace through the Plan de Iguala. This combination of forces illustrates the predominance of conventional form (the Plan de Iguala called for the establishment of a monarchy) similar in importance to Fernández de Lizardi's use of the traditional picaresque mode, a few years earlier. The victory won by the alliance did nothing to bring about a new order. Hidalgo and Morelos failed. Success came at last because "The clergy and the army, the priests, the landowners, and the minor officials — all, in fact, except the eighty thousand *gachupines* (Spaniards) — also wanted independence, but they wanted it without a war and without giving encouragement to the *mestizos* and the Indians" (Parkes 166).

Such disregard for the lower class is corroborated by the novels written after Mexico had won its national independence, and the absence of the poorest people is nowhere more conspicuous than in *El fistol del diablo*, published serially by Manuel Payno in 1845 and 1846. Whatever the shortcomings of this novel — and they are many — the author designed the narrative in such a way that many places in Mexico would be seen, and also many different segments of society. Given Payno's interest in exposing social problems, it is highly significant that the lower class plays no role; indeed, it never became a factor of great importance or of consistent interest in Mexican narrative or Mexican politics during the entire nineteenth century. The racially identified lower class became increasingly a problem to be ignored.

El fistol del diablo is the first novel after *El Periquillo Sarniento* to have the popular touch that would promise a continuation of Fernández de Lizardi's concern for "the people." Although it is not really a picaresque novel, Payno's narrative is enriched by a factor that may be described as a picaresque code, manifested in the satirical tone and the movement through a wide variety of social contexts. The major point of contact between the two novels is the call for common sense, the supposition that there must be a basis of reasonableness on which the society could operate. No less a personage than Satan himself enters the narrative to take a look at earthly foibles. Outstanding among the objects of criticism are the armies raised by individuals for the purpose of imposing their own views on the society in general. This kind of personalism characterized the years of the struggle for independence, and it continued into the national period.

Payno had sufficient reason for pointing out the futility of Mexican public policy following Independence. The time is commonly and rightly referred to as chaotic. In the simplest political terms, the struggle that evolved was between centralists and federalists, but this difference was complicated by various nuances that affected the positions of both conservatives (centralists) and liberals (federalists), e.g., whether Mexico was to be a monarchy or a centralist republic. The matter of private armies was particularly bothersome because it also involved regional differences, especially between the northern and southern regions of Mexico. The federal army was naturally, and usually, on the side of centralism. The church and the military emerged as the dominant forces in the new nation. While the church continued to amass wealth, the army's regional commanders acted as if centralism applied to everyone but the military, and they continued exercising the same freedom to exploit the populace that they had been allowed during the war with Spain. And if the centralist government should fail to accommodate their need (desire) for salaries and promotions, they might well initiate a *coup* in support of the opposition party.

> The thirty years which followed Independence was to be the era of the *pronunciamento*, and of the *cuartelazo*, or barrack revolt. A group of generals, led by a *caudillo*, would "pronounce" against the government, compose a "plan" denouncing it with an abundance of patriotic rhetoric and promising reform, and by offering to share the rewards of victory would frequently seduce any forces which might be sent against it (Parkes 178).

In addition to the threat of an army *coup, guerilleros* gathered under the command of regional *caciques* who were quite capable of being as unscrupulous as the generals, though such was not always the case. In its best moments, *caciquismo* probably favored the less privileged class — at least in rural areas — more than the government was disposed to do. However that may have been, it was hardly conducive to a stable society. And then there was the problem of Texas.

Among the disruptive forces in Mexican society of the time, none could surpass Antonio López de Santa Anna. His combination of opportunism, ambition, and organizational ability made him a dominant figure in the social context that also produced *El fistol del diablo*. Santa Anna was in and out of power several times, alternately the savior and the despair of his country. This paradoxical identity holds true even of his role in Mexico's war with the United States, significantly enough, because that war was a kind of climax to the period of chaos.

It is important to remember that Manuel Payno was presumably writing, and certainly publishing, *El fistol del diablo* as a serious novel, during the war. Two of the novel's more important characters lose their lives in action against the invasion by the United States. Certainly Payno's novel reflects the social conditions of its time, so one could hardly make a case for its anticipating a political change. The narrative criticizes specific problems — the penal system, for example —, some more general shortcomings of society, like the prevalence of opportunism, and the unattractive individual faults like avarice or lechery that are standard negatives during the Romantic Period. *El fistol del diablo* does belong to that period, in spite of certain realistic touches. One of its several plot lines involves a campaign waged by two young men to rescue a young woman from the clutches of a despicable old man. The combination of such standard fare with specifically Mexican problems is similar to Fernández de Lizardi's combination of the picaresque mode with ideological expositions related to his particular time and place.

One might think of Payno's extremely complicated narrative — interwoven plots and sub-plots — as analogous to the lines of political thought and action at that time in Mexico's history. Even the manner of publication (serial form in which structure and thematic consistency were reduced to a position of minor importance) might be taken as a reflection of the political chaos. Perhaps these qualities suggest a continuation of the same; only if one considers them a cry of desperation can they be associated with the Reform movement led by Benito Juárez. Taking an even darker view, one might say that many of the problems reflected by *El fistol del diablo* were so ingrained that not even the Reform movement would correct them.

The point of entry into the period of the Reform was really a span of about five years following the war with the United States, when Mexico was relatively peaceful or, perhaps better said, exhausted. In the middle of the eighteen-fifties, a new law requiring the sale of church and corporate properties was promulgated. This clearly innovative policy might have offered the hope of decreasing the power of the church and of effecting a desirable distribution of property among individual owners. In reality, the law had an adverse effect by attracting a new group of foreign investors and by generally favoring people who were already wealthy. The attempts at workable legislation continued, culminating in the constitution of 1857. This document was intended to provide for a democratic society and capitalistic development. Its most immediate effect, however, was radical cleavage between clericalist conservatives and anti-clerical liberals. The provisions intended to limit the power of the church were so severe that clerical authorities denied ministration of the sacraments to supporters of the constitution. On the other hand, such support was required of officeholders. The ensuing struggle between conservatives and liberals led to a civil war that lasted three years (1857-1860), the invasion by the French army (1862), the imposition of Maximilian (1864-1867), and the restoration of the republic under Juárez (1867). This is the period known as the Reform (and the Intervention). At several points during these years, there were indications of possible hope for the least privileged, but when all is said and done, the Reform was a bourgeois revolution. In theory, the movement should have produced a less fragmented society than the one portrayed in *El fistol del diablo*, but in fact, bitterness and divisiveness continued, as if Payno's novel had been a prediction of things to come, rather than a reflection of its immediate context. Charles C. Cumberland points out the "wanton destruction" practiced by both liberals and conservatives, and notes that desperation caused Juárez to take the most extreme anti-clerical measures (confiscation of church properties, suppression of monasteries, compulsory civil marriage) in 1859 (186). Cumberland's evaluation of this time is especially interesting, because he sets the futility of it against its more generally understood heroic quality. When all is said and done, the Reform was a consummately romantic movement. It was inspired by the notions of natural rights and individual human value. Its leaders thought it possible to organize a nation and, by so doing, make effective the common sense that Fernández de Lizardi and Payno had found lacking in Mexican society. That is not what happened. The forces of Juárez won the war, but the conservatives did not give up. They promoted the French Intervention and the empire under Maximilian. On the other hand, Juárez was not easily dissuaded either. Virtually in exile within his own country, he moved his government from place to place until the French withdrew. Maximilian was defeated and executed in 1867. The standard denouement to this romantic interlude is the equally romantic international plea for clemency toward Maximilian. Less remembered is Maximilian's decree of death to all supporters of Juárez, in 1865.

During these years of turmoil, few novels were published. Indeed, many of the potential novelists — all good romantics — were often on the battlefield. Nevertheless, in 1861, during the brief interim between the Three Years War (the War of the Reform) and the French Intervention, there was some considerable activity in the publication of fiction, the most remarkable of which are two novels by Nicolás Pizarro Suárez, *El monedero* and *La coqueta*. It seems probable that publication of these books — or at least of one of them — may have been delayed by the circumstances of the time.

Altamirano states, in his comments on *El monedero*, that he had read a manuscript of it when its author was still a student (411-412).

With regard to technical innovation, Pizarro's novels offer little of interest. They are distinguished from the general run of romantic novels by the author's relative success in communicating ideas through characterization. This phenomenon does not seem related in any significant way to the political changes taking place at the time or in the immediate future, except insofar as it is related to the romantic individualism apparent in politics. (It corresponds, of course, to the value generally placed on the individual conscience/consciousness at this time, not just in Mexico, but throughout Western culture.) On the other hand, a number of thematic innovations are very important. The most striking is reference to model communities, in both novels. In *El monedero*, the protagonist comes upon a community of native Mexicans, established and advised by Padre Luis, a priest more concerned with helping the poor while they are on earth than in promising them a good life in the next world. It is important to note that this interpretation of the priest's role, clearly Reformist in nature, is similar to the concept of the "good priest" in Altamirano's *La Navidad en las montañas* (1870). Padre Luis' role is even more radically anti-establishment; he asks for, and receives, release from his vows, so he can be married. Some speculation about when the novel was actually written leaves undetermined its exact relationship to the implementation of Reformist ideas.

Information about the model community is not very detailed; mainly we know that it is a democratic society in which all members are taught to be responsible citizens and are expected to contribute to the general well-being of the community, just as they participate in making decisions that affect everybody. A corollary to the message stated by the existence of this community is the protagonist, Francisco Hénkel, a native who has been educated and established in life by a German benefactor. (The model of German orderliness is fairly frequent in Mexican fiction during the latter half of the nineteenth century.) The principle set forth by this combination of

German discipline and a democratic society responds to the best intentions of the Reformists and their liberal predecessors. Another aspect of the same complex of liberal ideas — disdain for the *gachupines* — is embodied in Don Diego Díaz de Dávila, a caricature of persons who feign superiority by adopting Spanish customs and language characteristics.

El monedero is set during the United States' military intervention. Pizarro's second novel, *La coqueta*, is set during the Three Years War (War of the Reform), when President Juárez was in the city of Veracruz. The narrative incorporates a defense of the constitution of 1857, expressed mainly in expositions by Andrés, the protagonist, and exemplified in a priest's refusal to administer last rites to Andrés unless the latter will renounce the constitution. Pizzaro enhanced the feeling of immediacy and verisimilitude by using a real person, Juan Díaz Covarrubias, as an incidental character in the novel. (The real Díaz Covarrubias, a novelist/physician, was murdered by the conservatives, a short while after the time-setting of *La coqueta*, following the battle of Tacubaya, when he and other medical interns went to the battlefield to care for the wounded.)

While the projection of Reformist ideas is a very substantial factor in the experience of reading *La coqueta*, and probably make this novel more directly relevant to the political situation than any other Mexican novel up to that time, the work is imbued with romanticism and, therefore, is based on a story of love and tragedy, with an expected degree of improbability. This quality has little to do with the political situation except insofar as romantic improbability may be analogous to the very slight chance the Reformists had of realizing their dream. However, the love plot in this particular novel involves a view of the rights of women that is important, not only with reference to the political situation at the time (Pizarro advocates individual rights in all social contexts), but as an early manifestation of the emancipation of women.

The title of the novel, *La coqueta* (The Coquette), suggests a generally recognized type whose dominant characteristic is frivolity — a type that evolves into the merry, unattainable, demigoddess of *modernismo*. In Pizarro's narrative, Andrés is invited to the home of Magdalena, a famous coquette, and discovers that her flirtations are based not on fickleness, but on her resentment of custom that limits the rights of women in choosing partners. This characterization takes on increased importance in view of the development of a strong female character in another novel published the same year, *Vulcano*, by Hilarión Frías y Soto. In this connection, one should also note the defense of women's intelligence in Manuel Balbontín's *Memorias de un muerto* (1874), where this theme is again related to the qualities of an ideal society. In this novel, a major political principle is a presidential term of one year, with no reelection. One wonders whether Balbontín's principle was a commentary on the Juárez regime (Juárez was accused of dictatorial ambitions when he sought and won a fourth term in 1871), or a warning related to the coming dictatorship of Porfirio Díaz.

The model communities in Pizarro's novels are based on a democratic ideal that is hardly surprising for the time, but the manner of presentation is rather strange. What we know of the community in *El monedero* is told largely through letters from Padre Luis to Fernando. In *La coqueta*, the reference to a model community comes in an epilogue. After the end of the main story, the narrator skips three years to show what happened to the principals. We find Andrés, with wife and children, living on a farm that he owns and operates on a democratic basis. The displaced position of these model communities, in relation to the basic story lines, seems to separate them from the mainstream, suggesting the continued failure of attempts to implement the political ideal. To this extent, Pizarro's novels do forecast the frustration of Reformist policies — a condition which one may not refer to, accurately, as political change, but rather must see as the failure of an attempted change. When Juárez returned to Mexico City in 1867, he was a national hero, the defender of the constitution. In some ways, he continued to develop that image, but practical politics intervened. Troubles with the congress caused him to "safeguard himself by interfering with elections" (Parkes, 278), and soon the accusation of dictatorship arose. Juárez won reelection in 1871. He put down a rebellion by Porfirio Díaz, but died of a heart attack in 1872. Sebastián Lerdo de Tejada, an eminent intellectual though a poor politician, became president. When he announced for reelection in 1876, Díaz rebelled again, and won. Under the banner of "Universal Suffrage, No Reelection," he manipulated the vote and caused himself to be elected repeatedly (with the exception of one four-year interval) from that time until the Revolution -- a period of more than thirty years. So, practical politics suspended the dream of the Reform, a dream that existed on the periphery of Mexican reality, just as the model communities function marginally in Pizarro's narratives.

More optimistically, a thematic detail of *El monedero* recounts the reconstruction of the model community following its destruction by the novel's villain. This aspect of the narrative indicates the author's conscious belief in the persistence of democratic principles. On the other hand, his narrative strategy, since it displaces the community from the mainstream, more likely corresponds to his subconscious, instinctual evaluation of the social context.

There was plenty of reason for doubt, subconscious or otherwise. The interplay of villains and victims pervades the novels of the time. They portray a morally corrupt society, and register complaints similar to those in *El Periquillo Sarniento* or *El fistol del diablo*. With respect to model communities, José María Roa Bárcena wrote a specifically negative story in *La quinta modelo* (apparently written in 1857, though I do not know an edition earlier than 1870). This short novel is set in "184-", possibly with reference to one of the administrations of José Joaquín Herrera. Herrera, a general often described by historians as "mild-mannered," held the presidency for a year in 1844, and had been willing to negotiate the independence of Texas, prior to the war with the United States. After the war, he was returned to the presidency. He was a "moderado," an apparently good choice for the time; his regime was honest enough, but was ineffective with regard to controlling the enterprising and power-hungry *caciques* in the provinces.

The *récit* of Roa Bárcena's novel begins when Gaspar, the liberal protagonist, returns to Mexico because his political party has regained power. He enters politics and is made to look foolish by the author, because of his empty oratory and willing concession to those who use him for their own purposes. He ruins his son by enrolling him in a secular school, and almost destroys the happiness of his wife and daughter. He turns his farm into a model democratic community that will not function because the peons know nothing of democracy. Even worse, the novel informs us that they are uneducable, when Gaspar's son institutes a program of adult education. Conditions on the farm worsen to the point of anarchy, and the peons invade Gaspar's house. When a cleric comes to restore order, we realize that the authority favored by the author is not simply a conservative political system, but the Church itself.

There are no subtleties of structure that could likely alter the message of *La quinta modelo*. Although it is set in the eighteen-forties, its message, in general, seems eminently appropriate for a conservative in 1857, the first year of the War of the Reform. However, there is one detail — the program of adult education — that makes the 1857 date suspect; or, if that date is indeed correct, Roa Bárcena may have been anticipating Juárez's program of public education instituted upon the restoration of the republic. Education for the native Mexicans was a prime consideration of Juárez. Parkes reports that he once said he favored Protestantism because its clergy would have taught the people to read rather than to spend their money on votive candles (279). He entrusted his program of education to a commission headed by Gabino Barreda who had studied the Positivism of Auguste Comte. It is certain that this philosophical turn in Mexican education did little to help the native Mexicans. It is equally certain that it would be anathema to Roa Bárcena, a respected conservative who later supported Maximilian and was probably astonished, as were many others, by the emperor's liberalism. Interestingly enough, upon the restoration of the republic, following the withdrawal of the French and the defeat of Maximilian, Roa Bárcena collaborated with Altamirano and other liberals on *El Renacimiento*, an important literary magazine. The fact that such a collaboration was possible emphasizes the common desire among many writers, both liberal and conservative, to make a national literature in accord with a fresh start in the political realm.

Among the few novels that were published during the period of the empire, it is possible to find an interesting though hardly surprising contrast between anti-clericalism and the defense of religion. However, the novel that has always been considered most significant is Luis G. Inclán's *Astucia* (1865) or, to use its full title, *Astucia, el jefe de los hermanos de la hoja, o los charros contrabandistas de la rama*. The most interesting innovation of this novel is its praise of outlaws. The protagonist heads a company engaged in contraband, and their activities take place on the periphery of legitimate social organization. Small wonder that Altamirano, when he wrote his observations on the Mexican novel, completely ignored *Astucia*. It was hardly the kind of literature favored by a critic who believed the novel should be a constructive force in society. Within the *récit* of *Astucia*, however, the protagonist's decision to join the contrabandists is approved by his father when the latter discovers that his son has already given his word. This code of honor is manifested in many different episodes, and combines with characteristics of rural speech to give Inclán's work a special place in Mexican literary history. Its rural quality conferred a certain authenticity upon it, in the midst of novels that were almost always urban and usually imitative of European fiction, in both theme and technique.

In structure, *Astucia* is similar to most romantic novels: an intricate pattern of plot and subplots. Its principal storyline recounts, for the most part, battles between *los hermanos* (the "good guys") and two sets of "bad guys": (1) another, less honorable, company of smugglers and (2) the officers of the law. This narrative line is interrupted from time to time by the story of one or another of the *hermanos*. These subplots are related, sometimes awkwardly, to the main storyline, but they are more typical of romantic fiction, emphasizing moral corruption of an individual nature: infidelity, prostitution, deceit. The theme that relates all the subplots to the main story is the unwavering honor of the *hermanos*. The basis of this honor is loyalty to the specific group, with little concern for society as a whole. Sometimes a member's fidelity to this code runs counter to the law of the land, which is clearly considered to be relatively unimportant. Such an attitude exemplifies rather well one of Mexico's fundamental problems — before the publication of *Astucia* and after that time as well. It is this attitude that made effective government impossible. Given the condition that personal allegiance was more important than civic responsibility, it is quite natural that *caciquismo* flourished. Strong leaders could even seize the central power, but still not be able to organize the disparate elements of the nation. This problem is apparent in *El fistol del diablo*, for example, a novel which indicates the need for correction. The difference between Payno's novel and *Astucia* is that the latter seems to praise unlawfulness. The political innovation represented by the Reform movement was intended to bring order out of chaos. Consequently, *Astucia* projects a kind of anti-patriotism quite contrary to Reformist ideals and must have displeased those favoring greater social stability.

The work of Altamirano is important both for its thematic material (especially in *La Navidad en las montañas*, 1870) and for its structure (especially in *Clemencia*, 1869). The author was also important as a public figure, a Reformist who was active in politics and in battle, but is remembered especially for his promotion of literature. One can say that he was to literature what Juárez was to politics. Specifically, his greatest contributions were (1) founding *El Renacimiento*, (2) writing an account of the Mexican novel up to his time, and (3) providing a model of coherent narrative structure.

La Navidad en las montañas, probably the most widely read of Altamirano's works, possesses the nostalgic appeal of a Christmas celebration in an isolated village. It is not exactly a novel, but rather an extensive narrative sketch. A Reformist officer, on his way home after the war, meets a priest who invites him to spend Christmas Eve in a mountain village. Within this basic scheme, Altamirano incorporates the love story when a young man returns to the village on the night of the officer's visit. The primary storyline allows Altamirano the opportunity to set forth his views on religion, especially with respect to the good priest who is reminiscent of Padre Luis in Pizarro's *El monedero*: social justice is the desirable goal of religious activity. This principle is clearly in accord with Juárez's anti-clericalism; that is, traditional religious practice seemed irrelevant to the worldly needs of the people. He considered public education much more important.

The love story in *La Navidad en las montañas* is less oriented toward ideological expression, but it does allow criticism of the *leva*, a military draft that allowed communities to send young men to the army as a form of punishment. This practice is frequently portrayed as abhorrent, in novels published after *La Navidad en las montañas*.

Altamirano's structuring of this narrative enabled him to express some important opinions in ways that would not likely cause readers to object. However, it is in *Clemencia*, published a year earlier, that one can most clearly appreciate his awareness of novel structure. The care with which he made chapters of logical units of narrative, and the relative complexity of the narrative voice, are considerably more modern than the carelessly organized, ball-of-yarn narratives that were often published serially by his predecessors. It is also quite different from the series of episodes strung together by a picaro.

Clemencia is a story of love and patriotism, set in the historical context of the evacuation of Guadalajara, during the French intervention. Development of the *récit* contrasts the characters of two young officers in the federal army, one attractive in every way, the other quiet, rather homely. The latter turns out to embody values that Altamirano admired: courage, honor, compassion; the superficially gifted officer is found to be a traitor. Certainly this story is not striking for its originality. However, the narrative is different from earlier Mexican novels because the author does not complicate it with subplots. There is also a degree of restraint to his romanticism that creates an effect more melancholy than declamatory.

The narrative situation in *Clemencia* defines the act of narrating in such a way that the novelist supposes his reader will believe the story is true. The *récit* opens with the narrating voice explaining that some friends were gathered for dinner in the home of a physician. It was raining at the time of departure, so the host invited his guests to stay, conversing in his library. They noticed, on the wall, a quotation from the *Tales of Hoffman* that becomes, in effect, an epigraph to the story of the two officers. The physician, when asked about the quotation, explained that it referred to a story that he knew to be true and that he was willing to relate while they waited for the rain to stop. The *récit*, from that point, develops the storyline of love and patriotism (narrated by the physician), with rather detailed background information concerning the Intervention and the military situation that required the evacuation of Guadalajara. The physician-narrator tells, retrospectively, the story in which he was a minor character. He is able to delegate the narrating voice briefly to another character within the time frame of the love/patriotism storyline, but his own narrating position is set later, at the time of the dinner party. His narrative is fairly long, and at the end of the novel, "El Autor" signs a note in which he begs his readers to allow the novelist license to distort time, pointing out that, obviously, such a long story could not be told in one evening.

Altamirano's awareness of the act and art of narrating, his careful working out of the narrative situation, and the attention paid to cause and effect in the development of the conflict, all correspond to the Reformists' expectation of a well-ordered society. In fact, such a society did prevail superficially during the Díaz regime, though without the characteristics of justice and equality that Altamirano might have preferred. On the other hand, the novelist may have guessed that he might be forced to settle for less, since the outcome of *Clemencia* praises the values that Altamirano admired, but the fictional embodiment of them does not end up as winner, in any practical sense. The hero sacrifices himself for the happiness of someone else who, in turn, is totally distressed. Though it may appear strange, at first, to think of Altamirano as the author of a narrative that anticipated the characteristics of the Díaz regime, the correspondence is inescapable. If the political rhetoric of Diaz proposed effective suffrage and no re-election, the practical policy of his government was the imposition of peace and order. Here, indeed, was a political innovation realized. Whatever one may think of the Díaz regime taken as a whole, it certainly provided greater political stability than the nation had ever enjoyed. The careful structure of *Clemencia* anticipates this organization. Altamirano's care and insight with regard to the act of making a novel corresponds equally well to the political concern about how to govern. The fact is, however, that peace and order were maintained by the government at the cost of basic liberties, and below the surface of stability, peace was less than constant. Rebellions, banditry, and strikes persisted and were suppressed until suppression became impossible. It is this disarray below the surface that seems to be foreshadowed by the practical defeat of Altamirano's ideals (in the form of the hero) in *Clemencia*. One may argue, of course, that these ideals achieve a spiritual victory. That is part of the novel's melancholy romanticism; spiritual victory does not correspond to any aspect of practical politics.

Altamirano proposed that the novel could be used for the improvement of society, and he also urged the use of recognizably Mexican subject matter. This second recommendation may have been a factor in encouraging the writing of historical novels during the rest of the nineteenth century. As for the first proposition, it seems that Altamirano had in mind a complex of patriotism, progress, justice, loyalty, and cooperation. Unfortunately, the novelists who might have been influenced by him seem to have preferred themes like conjugal infidelity, miserliness, extortion, or similar matters related to personal morals rather than to collective social responsibility.

The novelist who probably came closest to doing what Altamirano suggested was José Tomás de Cuéllar, in a series of short novels that bear the general title of *La linterna mágica*. The original series was published in 1871 and 1872; they were published again, with the addition of five titles, from 1889 to 1892. A tendency toward realism becomes apparent in contrasting the earlier novels with the later ones. However, realism in Mexico involved the combination of two concepts: (1) realism like that of the *costumbrista* sketches (and more distantly, the picaresque novel), and (2) realism of the Flaubertian kind. Most of his novels are satirical portrayals of types, e.g., the *pollo* (irresponsible young blade), the *mariditos* (people who marry before they are mature enough to accept the concomitant responsibility), the *jamona* (overweight, gossipy woman), the *fuereños* (provincials recently arrived in the capital). Cuéllar deals with the lower middle class and, though he shows a certain amount of sympathy for his characters, he emphasizes their foolishness. Again one finds the plea for common sense, which differs slightly from Altamirano's melancholy search for practical comportment, but anticipates similar results. It is significant that Cuéllar controls the narrative completely; his satirical approach is not amenable to narrator displacement as in Altamirano's *Clemencia* (Brushwood 1966, 105-109). The behavior of Cuéllar's characters emphasizes once again the absence of common sense among the people. It certainly does not say much for Juárez's system of public education, or for the effect of Positivism. On the other hand, the Comtian ideas proposed by Gabino Barreda seem to have influenced the power elite, as Díaz depended more and more on his circle of *científicos*, the presidential advisers.

The kind of *costumbrista* narrative cultivated by Cuéllar is also found in Emilio Rabasa's *La guerra de tres años* (1891). This novel is a concise statement of a message set forth by the same author in four earlier works: the laws of the Reform were not appropriate to the needs of the populace. Such an attitude was supportive of the Díaz dictatorship which paid lip service to the principles of the Reform, but exercised political expediency at the expense of democracy, while favoring the wealthy and ignoring the existence of the poor. The main point in *La guerra de tres años* turns on a matter of traditional religious practice. A local official, implementing the prohibitions set by the laws of the Reform, will not allow a religious procession. The citizens demand it, and higher authorities resolve the problem by transferring their local representative to another locale and allowing the procession to take place. This representation is both reflective and predictive; anti-clerical laws have never been entirely effective in Mexico. Rabasa's novel, in its statement

about practical politics and by its use of the very traditionalist picaresque code, corresponds to the politics of the Díaz regime.
With respect to the culture in general, Rabasa's novel lacks the
Gallic element that became so prominent in the latter part of the
nineteenth century. This difference simply emphasizes the two aspects of realism in Mexico. Other novels are closer to the Flaubertian variety. The latter are more innovative, in a sense, because
they do not adhere to the Hispanic tradition. However, the general
orientation of Mexican culture, and of life among the more privileged sectors of society, was French. So one may say that, in a different sense, the advent of Flaubertian realism was routine and expected.

Tomochic (1895), by Heriberto Frías, shows the author's awareness of both realism and naturalism. It may also be the most innovative Mexican novel of the nineteenth century. Thematically, it
revealed the weakness of the Díaz regime when faced by determined opposition. This crack in the wall of dictatorial authority
was underlined by variations in the narrative voice that allowed the
expression of clearly anti-establishment sentiments.

Tomochic is based on the last of the federal army's three cam-
paigns to put down the rebellion of an indigenous community in
northern Mexico. The first two expeditions met with inglorious defeat; the third overwhelmed the rebels by force of numbers, burned
the town, and killed the men. This narrative of action is accompanied by a love story (the romantic idea of a love interest as a *sine
qua non* dies hard) that had little effect on the way Frías' novel was
regarded by the establishment. In spite of the fact that the basic
narrator (an obvious *alter ego* of Frías, who actually took part in the
third expedition), praises the federal army, the overall effect of this
praise is ironic because one senses a relentless current of doubt,
among the soldiers, regarding the task they are assigned. *El
Demócrata*, an opposition newspaper, began the serial publication
of *Tomochic* in 1893. Before it was completed, the newspaper was
closed down and Frías was arrested on a charge of having revealed
military secrets. The charge was ludicrous; the only military secret

revealed in *Tomochic* was that the federal army was vulnerable because the soldiers were not eager to murder civilians.

Frías' novel has come to be generally regarded, and justifiably so,
as a precursor to the novel of the Mexican Revolution. It was certainly one of several works that strongly suggested the probability
of political change; however, the others did not communicate their
message as directly, at least to members of the establishment.

Federico Gamboa's first full-length novel, *Suprema ley* (1896), is
probably the best example of naturalism in Mexican fiction. Innovative in this sense, it is also notable for having made even greater
use of variable narrative voice than *Tomochic*. Analysis of this process reveals an interesting conflict between traditionalism and
change — one that would not be apparent to a casual reader, especially in view of the author's conservative politics. Gamboa belonged to a conservative family, supported the Díaz dictatorship,
even served in the government of Victoriano Huerta, the
anti-revolutionary strong man who took over the position of power
after the murder of Madero. In fairness to Gamboa, one should
note that more than a few Mexicans supported Huerta because
they saw his regime as a path away from chaos. Nevertheless, the
novelist Gamboa would be most surprised to know that any reader
had found one of his narratives to be in any way suggestive of
change from the established order.

Suprema ley is a story of adultery in which Julio follows in-
eluctably the naturalist path to desolation and death while Clotilde,
his partner in adultery, is redeemed. By representing the characters in different ways, beginning with their initial appearances in
the novel, Gamboa makes their disparate fates seem reasonable.
In so doing, he portrays the judicial system as inadequate, even
ridiculous. This fact is entirely in accord with Gamboa's general
ideas; he saw shortcomings in the bureaucracy even though he supported the regime.

The most impressive aspect of *Suprema ley*, with regard to the
conflict between traditionalism and change, centers on an episode,
after Julio has deserted his family, in which his son is reading a romantic novel to his mother, the forsaken woman. The narrator

refers to the novel in terms that are not at all complimentary. Yet, ironically, the destiny of Julio's family, from that time on, follows a course suggestive of the novel that mother and son were reading. Julio, on the other hand, deteriorates steadily and rapidly. The new kind of fiction that Gamboa learned to cultivate seems to have trapped him. He appears to deprecate the traditionalism of Julio's family. At the same time, Julio, a possible representative of change, can come to no good end. Perhaps that is the prediction of the conservative Gamboa: that change in Mexico was doomed to failure. Whatever the communication of this strange situation, *Suprema ley* certainly suggests change, in the same degree that one finds the suggestion in Gutiérrez Nájera or in Nervo — a kind of preliminary hint of the will to change that took shape unmistakably in the work of the Ateneo, that intellectual side of the Revolution.

Chapter Five

Conclusions

Recognition of analogies between two of society's constituent factors (narrative and politics, in the case of this study) invites a search for analogies with other such factors, especially the fine arts. In the preceding chapters, some rather superficial references to painting have been useful. It is probable that all other constituent factors would be analogous — even those that are less fundamental to the human enterprise than creative art, e.g., education, banking, the institutional church. It is reasonable to suppose that change occurs in all these components of society at more or less the same time. On a carefully measured chronological scale, one or another of the factors may be identified as the first of several to reveal innovative qualities that may be seen later as basic to the analogy.

At least in theory, one may suppose a chronologically progressive list of social components that participate in analogical correspondence. Such careful measurement, however, seems pointless because there is no way to show that innovation in (or by) one constituent factor *causes* innovation in (or by) another. In other words, the study of analogy is concerned with correspondence, not with cause and effect. In the course of social change, the observation of some innovative activity in any of society's components will suggest that similar innovation is occurring elsewhere, but establishment of a presumed order, or identification of the exact nature of the analogy, would be highly speculative.

It does seem that analogous innovations will occur, whether they are spontaneous within the culture under examination or imported from another culture and adapted to the local one. The popular music and literature of the nineteen-sixties in Mexico provide a good illustration of adaptation. Music identified with the youth of that period often came from England, where it had grown on the basis of an import from the United States; in other instances, it came from the United States, where it was re-imported from England. This music found a place in many national cultures, and an international study of the phenomenon might be instructive. In Mexico, there is an obvious analogy between "rock" and the narrative of the "onda." The relationship between these fictions and political activism is obvious enough. One might suppose also that some of the writers of the "onda" knew the novels of J. D. Salinger and Robert Gover. However, nothing about such relationships makes the novels of the "onda" less innovative, in the context of Mexican culture.

It is especially interesting, in the present study, to see how often narrative innovation in the twentieth century precedes an analogous change in politics. One finds that narrative is less likely to anticipate painting. This fact suggests that one or another of the creative arts may regularly provide the initial point of innovation. Such a condition would not be surprising, if one turned away from the pragmatic daily routine and confronted what is often suspected though never quite recognized: that creative artists, by a combination of innate desire, professional preparation, and insistent observation, may regularly function a step ahead — or even several steps ahead — of the game of social organization that we regularly play.

If the foregoing seems more speculative than conclusive, one may be able to fasten onto certain ideas by specific reference to the present study of narrative and politics. It has become apparent, in the course of analysis, that different *levels* of analogy must be observed — levels, that is, differentiated by degrees of refinement. For example, the multiple changes and overlapping tendencies in narrative during the vanguardist period of the nineteen-twenties and nineteen-thirties are analogous to the political search for an appropriate post-Revolutionary politics. This is a rather gross analogy as contrasted with the proposition that the pro-Hispanism of the *colonialista* novel is analogous to the turn away from radical nativism/agrarianism on the part of the Calles regime. The difference in levels can be seen here by contrasting the two analogies. The second is contained within the first; it is a sub-analogy based on details contained within the larger proposition. In each case, the literary factor precedes its political analogue in time, but the difference in degree of refinement makes the crossing of elements between the two analogies meaningless. In other words, the two analogies, though related, are not metaphors of each other. It is not meaningful to say that the multiple changes and overlapping tendencies in narrative during the vanguardist period are analogous to the turn away from radical nativism/agrarianism on the part of the Calles government. It would be equally meaningless to say the pro-Hispanism of the *colonialista* novel is analogous to the search for an appropriate post-Revolutionary politics. Care must be practiced with respect to such differences of level. Although there is no apparent objective way of determining the level, one can at least test the metaphoric possibility. If the elements in two related analogies are interchangeable, both analogies are operating on the same level; one is not subordinate to the other.

When analogies are studied, the possibility of prediction naturally comes to mind. A cautious response to this suggestion is the only advisable one. With respect to narrative and politics, one might prefer not to take innovation in one as a means of predicting change in the other. However, given a context with certain characteristics, narrative innovation does provide ground for interesting speculation. The present study certainly offers ample evidence to refute the commonly held notion that prose fiction only reflects its social context. Words like "predict" and "forecast," as they have been used here, may mislead some readers, since they may connote causation. The most satisfactory word (one tires of using it always) is "presage," because it can suggest foreshadowing, the fact that one constituent of society may reveal certain qualities before the other constituents do, without being a causative force.

In Mexico, narrative innovation immediately preceding and following the military phase of the Revolution seems to have marked a radical change in the reflective-versus-anticipatory role of fiction. The political change effected by the Revolution (even its most fundamental innovation — that is, change itself, without qualification) seems to have been anticipated, in various ways, by narrative innovation. Since that time, narrative has almost always been an earlier indicator of change. In the preceding century, it is easy to see how narrative reflected political change, but much harder to make a case for narrative as forerunner. One must recognize the possibility, in this connection, that the creative arts were disenthralled, so to speak, by the Revolution and, therefore, were able to exercise more fully their natural capacities. Or it may be that this difference between the nineteenth and twentieth centuries was created by disparity in the volume of narrative available for study. The novel was not a widely cultivated genre in Mexico prior to the middle of the nineteenth century. A steady increase is notable from the time of the restoration of the republic. However, the very nature of the Díaz dictatorship not only reduced the probability of change of any kind, it tended to co-opt the novelists of the period.

In general, the change of which the Revolution was a part may be described as corresponding to the desire to be modern. In applying the observations made in this study to an analysis of a different national culture, one might begin by asking the following two questions:

1. Is there a point in the history of narrative fiction, written in a given national culture, when the narrative, generically speaking, appears determined to be modern —-- that is, either to be as up-to-date as the narrative of some other national culture, or to be consciously different from an accepted canon?

2. Does the desire to be modern appear related to a political change?

Obviously, these questions make sense only in contexts where narrative is cultivated extensively, in a period and place when and where the writing of prose fiction is/was considered a desirable artistic enterprise.

Nineteenth-century Mexico does not offer rich possibilities, but can be interesting nonetheless. The case of Altamirano is especially so because, at first glance, his narratives seem to reflect, and only reflect. But on more careful consideration, one finds some suggestions of things to come. Quite different is the chapter on vanguardism, in part because it has been necessary to look backward and note narrative anticipation of the Revolution, in order to explain the extraordinary happenings of the nineteen-twenties. This fact makes for a rather complicated exposition of analogies, the most important of which is between (a) experimentation with various kinds of narrative and (b) experimentation with public policy. Leaving aside several more specific analogies observed within this period, an important secondary proposition, of a still rather general nature, is that the straightforward storytelling, in the *relato* of the Revolution, anticipated the populist/socialist orientation of the Cárdenas administration. With regard to the first major analogy, one might pose these questions:

1. Is there a period of experimentation when narrative seems to try many different techniques and themes within a short period of time?

2. Does this period of multiple experimentation in narrative correspond to or anticipate a period of political experimentation or instability?

With regard to the second analogy, one should notice that it is a reaction to the first. That is, the "straightforward narration" referred to above is more representational (verisimilar) in its projection of human experience, and it employs few of the techniques that serve novelists in the creation of special effects. Any narrative transforms its referent to some extent, and no quantitative specification is possible. But the *relato* of the Revolution stays close to what actually happened, makes little attempt to be artful. (Naturally, since there is no quantitative definition, the "straightforward storytelling" description admits relative differences.) This kind of narrative appeared while vanguardist experimentation was still practiced, and soon the representational became predominant. The assumption of the analogy is that the narratives referred to are accessible to a wider range of readership than vanguardist experimentation could possibly be, and that, for this reason, they anticipated the populist/socialist slant of the Cárdenas government. One might ask the following questions:

1. Is the period of experimentation followed by a reaction favoring simplicity in narration?

2. If so, does the return to simplicity precede a people-oriented political administration?

3. Does it anticipate a clearly defined political program?

Probably the most useful perception emanating from the chapter on internationalization is the phenomenon called "essentialization," a term invented to describe an act of narrating that creates a transcendent regionalism. That is, the narrative that deals with identifiably Mexican subject matter emphasizes what is generally human in this material, and uses modern techniques of narration that transform documentary reality into a complex of feelings that communicate the vitality of the circumstance to which the narrative refers. Essentialization of this kind is one of the phenomena observable in the culture's tendency to become internationalized. Its effect is the establishment of the nation's cultural identity within an international context. The analogy with governmental recognition of national roots via institutional activities is very apt. The founding of museums is a typical activity. By emphasizing the nation's ethnic qualities, its history, and its art, museums stimulate national self-awareness and, at the same time, serve as a kind of calling card for the country, within the international community. One might pose the following questions:

1. Is there a time when national (local) themes are developed in narratives by using experimental strategies of narration?

2. Does this quality correspond to or anticipate growing international obligations on the part of the government?

Several developments related to essentialization are important to the study of Mexico, but may not be universally applicable. For example, the erasure of defining lines (noticeable in painting as well as in narrative) corresponds to the essentialization of the Revolution itself. A new perception of this historical event led novelists to interpret it, rather than describe it. Recognition of the Revolution as an accomplished fact is certainly analogous to changing the name of the dominant political party from Partido de la Revolución Mexicana to Partido Revolucionario Institucional.

Internationalism also promoted the growth of urbanism, as most segments of society strove to reach higher levels of sophistication. Narrative fiction clearly moved in this direction. Relationship with Europe was an important consideration. There was an "Americanist" promotion that preceded, and then extended into, the period of Mexico's participation in World War II. The literary magazine *El Hijo Pródigo* stimulated a renewal of interest in Europe. Significantly, the magazine was founded after Mexico declared war on the axis powers — a clear case of public policy preceding the literary event. It is equally important to note that this political change was not generated internally, but was caused by influence from outside.

One of the most extraordinary analogies is between emphasis on multiple points of view as a narrative strategy and the convocation of former presidents as a political innovation. This pairing seems almost too pat to be credible, but it is a fact of history. Both phenomena suggest the movement toward technocracy and self-reference that is one of the most important considerations in the third chapter.

The basic principle dealt with in the chapter on rebellion and analysis has to do with two tendencies that look similar, on the one hand, and quite different, on the other: (1) the nonconformism of the "onda" and (2) self-conscious narrative. Novels that most likely fit the description of "self-conscious" are not characterized by the nonconformism of the "onda" novelists. However, the "onda" novelists reveal a strong predilection for self-conscious narrative, and both phenomena (nonconformism and self-consciousness) indicated the desire to change, with emphasis on the creative act. The "onda's" nonconformism did not anticipate an official political change, but it certainly forecast the political activism of 1968, and, in a strange way, presaged (even incited) the strong-armed repression that followed. At the same time, self-conscious narrative preceded bureaucratic emphasis on process, with busy-ness occupying the position of first priority. The following questions are pertinent:

1. Has the country experienced a period of youthful irreverence in narrative?

2. If so, did it anticipate either public demonstration or change in public policy?

3. Has the cultivation of self-referential narrative accompanied or anticipated increased committee investigations or reviews that delay decision making and the implementation of policy?

The questions set forth so far in these concluding statements are, of course, inversions of the assertions made in the preceding chapters. Therefore, the answers are affirmative with respect to Mexico, but they might produce a different result if the same or similar questions were asked about a different national culture. With regard to precedence — that is, whether change in narrative precedes or follows an analogous change in politics — one notes that narrative most often precedes in Mexico. Of course, it might be that some particularly Mexican set of circumstances encourages this sequence in the culture studied here. If that should be true, then the argument for some sort of prescience, on the part of novelists, would be considerably weakened. However, one should always remember that precedence is not related to cause and effect. All constituent factors of a society will demonstrate analogous characteristics, even though these characteristics may be apparent in one factor earlier than in another. For this reason, it is best to put aside the notion that novels reflect the society in which they are written, and grant, to the genre, the status of an organic component of the culture.

Having observed the function of a set of questions in the Mexican context, one may ask to what extent they may be generalized. Several propositions emerge and offer themselves for testing. Since all the propositions are based on narrative innovation, the point of departure must always refer to the creative act of writing fiction. One selects a moment when there is notable change in the cultivation of this genre. Then the following propositions may be considered:

1. A period of widely diverse, or rapidly changing innovations in narrative will be analogous to a period of confusion, or rapidly changing policies, in the realm of politics.

2. A predominance of straightforward storytelling (narrative in which interesting characters and simple plot structure dominate) will be analogous to a clearly oriented public policy, most likely tending to be concerned for the welfare of the less favored economic strata.

3. Narrative that essentializes the national characteristics through the use of simultaneity, erasure of defining line, or other techniques that transform fact into experience, will be analogous to a government with decidedly bourgeois tendencies that combine with programs for recognizing cultural roots (museums, research institutes, support for higher education, etc.)

4. Self-referential narrative will be analogous to a growing bureaucracy, ineffective administration, and rhetoric designed to
reassure the public that all is well.

5. An abundance of historical novels or personally nostalgic
novels will be analogous to a conservative, possibly repressive,
government.

Whether or not these prepositions are confirmed in the analysis of
a narrative/fiction relationship, the examination will necessarily
display interesting aspects of the culture under study, because
there will certainly be analogies, even though they may differ from
the propositions set out here. Inevitably, such a study will bring up
the matter of predictive capability. The only reason for expecting
narrative innovation to predict political change rests on the assumption of a kind of creative prescience produced by the authors'
combination of imagination, preparation, and observation. Even
this reason would not suppose narrative innovation to presage innovation in the other creative arts, but it would presumably suggest
that the creative arts reveal an innovative tendency before a corresponding change becomes apparent in other constituent factors of
the society. In Mexico, especially during the twentieth century, a
strong case can be made for narrative precedence. As extraordinary as this claim may seem to people who are used to thinking of
literary art as an addendum to society, it is fully as sensible as the
standard supposition that narrative fiction is only a reflection of its
context.

Works Cited

Anderson, Danny J. "Una aproximación a la metaficción: tres casos distintos en la novela mexicana contemporánea." *Semiosis*, 7-8 (Jul. - Dec., 1981, Jan. - Jun., 1982), 123-140.

Arévalo Martínez, Rafael. "Triángulo fatal." *Crisol*, 1 (Jan., 1929), 35-36.

Arias, Arturo. "Ideología y lenguaje en *Hombres de maíz*." *Texto Crítico*, XI, 33 (Sept-Dec., 1985), 153-164.

Arquin, Florence. *Diego Rivera: the Shaping of an Artist*. Norman: Oklahoma UP, 1971.

Azuela, Mariano. "La luciérnaga." *Contemporáneos*, 3 (Aug., 1928), 235-252.

———. "La luciérnaga. Capítulo final." *Contemporáneos*, 23 (Apr., 1930), 20-33.

———. "La malhora." *Contemporáneos*, 30-31 (Nov. - Dec., 1930) 193-216 and 32 (Jan., 1931), 42-70.

Barreda, Octavio G. "*Gladios, San-en-ank, Letras de México, El Hijo Pródigo.* In *Las revistas literarias de México*, la serie (México: INBA, 1963). Pp. 209-238.

Basáñez, Miguel. *La lucha por la hegemonía en México: 1968-1980*. México: Siglo XXI, 1981.

Bell, Steven M. "Literatura crítica y crítica de la literatura: teoría y práctica en la obra de Salvador Elizondo." *Chasqui*, XI, 1 (Nov., 1981), 41-52.

Bruce-Novoa, John. "La Generación de la Escritura y las artes visuales." *El Semanario Cultural de Novedades* (Apr. 24, 1988), 6-9.

Brushwood, John S. *Mexico In Its Novel*. Austin: Texas UP, 1966.

————. *"Contemporáneos* and the Limits of Art." *Romance Notes*, V, 2 (Spring, 1964), 1-5.

Camp, Roderic A. *Intellectuals and the State in Twentieth-Century Mexico*. Austin: Texas UP, 1985.

Campos, Marco Antonio. *Que la carne es hierba*. México: Mortiz, 1982.

————. *Señales en el camino*. México: Premiá, 1983.

Carballo, Emmanuel. *Protagonistas de la literatura mexicana*. Mexico: Ediciones del Ermitaño/SEP, 1986.

Carter, Boyd G. *Historia de la literatura hispanoamericana a través de sus revistas*. México: Ediciones de Andrea, 1968.

Colín, Eduardo. "Los de abajo." In Monterde, Francisco, ed. *Mariano Azuela y la crítica mexicana*. México: SepSetentas, 1973. Colin's review was published originally in *El Universal*, Jan. 30, 1925.

Cosío Villegas, Daniel. *Change in Latin America: the Mexican and Cuban Revolutions*. Lincoln: Nebraska UP, 1961.

Cuevas, José Luis. "The Cactus Curtain." Trans. by Lysander Kemp. *Evergreen Review*, 2, 7 (Winter, 1959), 111-120.

Cumberland, Charles C. *Mexico: the Struggle for Modernity.* New York: Oxford UP, 1968.

Dallal, Alberto. *La danza contra la muerte.* México: UNAM, 1979.

Debicki, Andrew P. *Antología de la poesía mexicana moderna.* London: Tamesis, 1977.

Forster, Merlin H. "Las novelas de Jaime Torres Bodet." *La Palabra y el Hombre* 9, no. 34 (1965), 207-212. [In the absence of this number of the periodical, this citation is taken from Schwartz, Kessel. *A New History of Spanish American Fiction.* Coral Gables: Miami UP, 1971, p. 359. The information about JTB's novel was taken from a copy of the manuscript which was later published in *La Palabra y el Hombre.*]

García Canclini, Néstor. "Los dilemas de las culturas populares latinoamericanas bajo la confluencia de tradición, modernidad y posmodernidad: el caso mexicano." Dittoed condensation in English of a lecture given at a seminar ("The Debate on Postmodernism in Latin America: Brazil, Mexico, and Peru") at the University of Texas, Austin, April 29-30, 1988.

García Flores, Margarita. *Aproximaciones y reintegros.* México: UNAM, 1982.

Genette, Gérard. *Narrative Discourse.* Trans. by Jane E. Lewin. Ithaca: Cornell UP, 1980.

Glantz, Margo. *Repeticiones: ensayos sobre literatura mexicana.* Jalapa: Universidad Vercruzana, Centro de Investigaciones Lingüístico-Literarias, 1979.

Gutiérrez Cruz, Carlos. "Arte y lucha social." *Crisol*, 1, (Jan., 1929), 27-30.

Icaza, Xavier. *Panchito Chapopote*. Xalapa, Ver.: Universidad Veracruzana, 1986.

——. *La revolución en la literatura*. México: Conferencias del Palacio de Bellas Artes, 1934.

Johnson, John J. *Political Change in Latin America*. Stanford: Stanford UP, 1958.

Kariel, Henry S. *Beyond Liberalism, Where Relations Grow*. San Francisco: Chandler and Sharp, 1977.

Kecskemeti, Paul. "Static and Dynamic Society." In Spitz, David (ed.). *Political Theory and Social Change*. New York: Atherton Press, 1958.

Koeniger, Patty. "Introduction" to *A Salute to Carlos Mérida*. Austin: University of Texas Art Museum, 1976.

Krauze, Enrique & Tajonar, Héctor. "El laberinto mexicano revisitado: nuestro Tiempo Nublado." *El Semanario Cultural de Novedades* (July 21, 1985), 1-2.

List Arbuzide, Germán. *El movimiento estridentista*. Jalapa, Ver.: Ediciones de *Horizonte*, 1927.

Martínez, José Luis. *Literatura mexicana siglo XX: 1910-1949*. Primera parte. México: Antigua Librería Robredo, 1949.

Meyer, Leonard B. *Music, the Arts, and Ideas*. Chicago: Chicago UP, 1967.

Mier, Luis Javier and Carbonell, Dolores. *Periodismo interpretativo: Entrevistas con ocho escritores mexicanos*. México: Trillas, 1981.

Monsiváis, Carlos. "Muerte y resurrección del nacionalismo mexicano." *Nexos*, 109 (Jan., 1987), 13-22.

Moussong, Lazslo. "La plenitud del hiperrealismo en Gelsen Gas." *México en el Arte*, 14 (otoño, 1986), 102-107.

Mullen, Edward J. *Contemporáneos: Revista mexicana de cultura*. (Salamanca/Madrid: Anaya, 1972).

––––––. "Salazar Mallen's *Cariátide*: A Forgotten Chapter in Mexican Literary History." In Vera, Catherine and McMurray, George R. (eds.). *In Honor of Boyd G. Carter* (Laramie: University of Wyoming, 1982).

Nervo, Amado. *Un epistolario inédito*. Prólogo y notas de Ermilo Abreu Gómez. México: Imprenta Universitaria, 1951.

Nodelman, Sheldon. *Marden, Novros, Rothko: Paintings in the Age of Actuality*. Houston: Rice U Institute of Arts, 1978.

Parkes, Henry Bamford. *A History of Mexico*. Boston: Houghton Mifflin, 1970.

Patán, Federico. "*Manifestación de silencios* y el '68." *Sábado*, supplement to *UnoMásUno* (Sept. 7, 1985) 7.

Paz, Octavio. *Hombres en su siglo y otros ensayos*. México: Seix Barral, 1984.

––––––. "Hora cumplida (1929-1985)." *Vuelta*, 103 (June, 1985), 7-12.

Pérez Firmat, Gustavo. *Idle Fictions*. Durham: Duke UP, 1982.

Picón Garfield, Evelyn and Schulman, Ivan A. "*Las entrañas del vacío*": *ensayos sobre la modernidad hispanoamericana*. México: Cuadernos Americanos, 1984.

Ramos, Samuel. *El perfil del hombre y la cultura en México*. Buenos Aires/México: Austral, 1952.

Revueltas, José. *El luto humano*. México: Era, 1980.

Reyes Palma, Francisco. "50 años de artes plásticas y política en México (1934-1984)," *Plural*, 200 (May, 1988), 34-44.

Rojas Garciadueñas, José. "El movimiento literario del 'colonialismo'." *Boletín del Instituto de Investigaciones Bibliográficas*, I, 1 (Jan.-Jun., 1969), 19-24.

———. *El Ateneo de la Juventud y la Revolución*. México: Biblioteca del Instituto Nacional de Estudios Históricos de la Revolución Mexicana, 1979.

Saavedra, Leonora. "50 años de música de concierto en México." *Plural*, 200 (May, 1988), 45-51.

Said, Edward W. "The Problem of Textuality: Two Exemplary Positions." In Phillipson, Morris & Gudel. *Aesthetics Today*. New York: New American Library, revised edition, 1980.

Salazar Mallén, Rubén. *Páramo*. No publisher; printed in México: Talleres de la Editorial Stylo, 1944.

Schmeckebier, Lawrence E. *Modern Mexican Art*. Minneapolis: Minnesota UP, 1939.

Schneider, Luis Mario. *El estridentismo: México, 1921-1927*. México: Universidad Nacional Autónoma de México, 1985.

Smith, Peter H. *Labyrinths of Power: Political Recruitment in Twentieth-Century Mexico*. Princeton: Princeton UP, 1979.

Strode, Hudson. *Timeless Mexico*. New York: Harcourt Brace, 1944.

Vargas, Margarita. *El grupo "Revista Mexicana de Literatura" y sus coetáneos: La narrativa*. Ph. D. dissertation, University of Kansas, 1985.

Vela, Arqueles. *El Café de Nadie*. Jalapa, Ver.: Ediciones de *Horizonte*, 1926.

Vogeley, Nancy. "The Concept of 'the People' in *El Periquillo Sarniento*." *Hispania* 70, 3 (Sept., 1987), 457-467.

Yañez, Agustín. *Al filo del agua*. México: Porrúa, 1955.

Zaid, Gabriel. "Escenarios sobre el fin del PRI." *Vuelta*, 103 (June, 1985), 13-21.

Zaitzeff, Serge I. "Julio Torri (1889-1970), Estudio Preliminar" and "Material bibliográfico." In Torri, Julio. *Diálogo de libros*. México: Fondo de Cultura Económica, 1980.

———. *El arte de Julio Torri*. México: Oasis, 1983.

Zermeño, Sergio. *México: una democracia utópica. El movimiento estudiantil del '68*. México: Siglo XXI, 1978.

University of Texas Studies
in Contemporary Spanish-American Fiction

Robert Brody
General Editor

This new series welcomes original critical studies (200-350 pp.) in English or Spanish on any aspect of the narrative literature in Spanish America from its formative period in the 1930s and 1940s to the present. No methodological approach will be excluded, provided the manuscript does not contain excessive technical terminology that might tend to obscure rather than illuminate.